Oriental Aesthetics

PLATE I. *A Poet-musician*. From the Tuti-Nama,
Folio 110 verso. Mogul, early reign of Abkar.
(Courtesy of The Cleveland Museum of Art).

ومقرب بنابد تا در نظر معشوق از رو با ضبطی در وجود نیاید ذهر انکه
علم موسیقی نیکو دانند تا معشوق را حضور او طرب نیز زیادت حاصل شود

قطعه

| جهل در ادبی جنون باشد | تخشبی ذوفنون شدن کار یت |
| در محمد من ذوفنون بّاشند | مرد کامل کسی بود امروز |

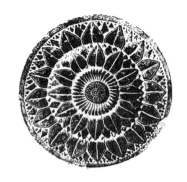

Thomas Munro

Oriental Aesthetics

The Press of Western Reserve University
Cleveland, Ohio

Acknowledgments

A preliminary outline of this book was presented at the Fifth International Congress on Aesthetics in Amsterdam on August 25th, 1964. Under the title, "Oriental Traditions in Aesthetics," it is scheduled for publication in the *Proceedings* of that Congress, edited by Professor Jan Aler, and also as an introduction to the special issue on Oriental aesthetics of the *Journal of Aesthetics and Art Criticism*, Fall 1965.

Thanks are extended to the Franklin J. Matchette Foundation of New York for timely aid in these efforts to develop more Western understanding of Far Eastern ideas about art; also to The Cleveland Museum of Art for supplying illustrative and reference material, for Dr. Merald Wrolstad's artistry in book design, and for Dolores Filak's expert secretarial work. I acknowledge with thanks permission to reprint the many short quotations from published writings for which credit is given in the notes. In particular, I am indebted for valuable references and suggestions to the following scholars in Oriental fields: Sherman E. Lee, Wai-kam Ho, and Margaret Marcus, of The Cleveland Museum of Art, and Donald J. Munro of the University of Michigan. However, these scholars are not to be held responsible for the controversial opinions expressed, or for any faults the book may contain.

T.M.

Contents

vii

viii

List of Illustrations

ix

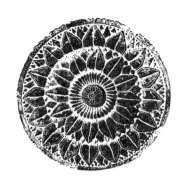

Part One

An Introductory Survey

1. The need for comparative study of Eastern and Western theories of art

This book is, first of all, a plea for more internationalism in aesthetics, especially between scholars in the West and the Far East. There is need for more active interchange of ideas and more cooperative research among aestheticians from opposite sides of the earth. Aesthetics as a subject of world-wide scope should be based on observations and ideas from all the major art-producing regions. The present gulf between Oriental and Occidental contributions to it should be more effectively bridged over. Scholars in each hemisphere could profit from a greater understanding of the best work done in the other.

Toward that end, Part One of this book presents a short introductory survey of some outstanding works on Oriental aesthetics, now available in English or some other European language. After a few preliminary comments on the present situation, it will emphasize traditional writings—roughly, those dating back over a century, especially the more ancient ones. It will mention both primary sources and recent interpretations of them. Geographically, it will be limited to India, China, and Japan. An unusually large number of bibliographical references and short quotations is included for the benefit of students and researchers.

Part Two will shift the emphasis to a brief interpretation and appraisal of Oriental aesthetics, especially as to its potential value for Western thought. It will also discuss the question whether a selective synthesis can be made of the best elements in Oriental and Occidental aesthetics. To what extent can they be reconciled? To what extent are they radically opposed?

Oriental theories of art are deeply permeated with a philosophy of religious mysticism which is largely unacceptable to naturalistic thinkers in the West. As we shall see, they also contain much wise generalization on the arts which is based on long empirical and practical experience. This can be separated from its mystical context and considered in its own right. Western aesthetics can learn much of value from it.

There are serious obstacles in the way of East-West cooperation in aesthetics. Languages and distances are major obstacles, of course. Few Western scholars can read Oriental texts in the original. A large-scale program is needed for the translation of important works on aesthetics, old and new, back and forth between the leading European and Asiatic languages of scholarship. But even after this is done, some difficult barriers will remain. Some of them are philosophic and religious differences of long standing. Ignoring them will not remove them. To point them out may help us to by-pass them.

The task of translating technical, theoretical writing into a very different language, to be read by people in an age and culture far from the original one, is obviously formidable. It calls for ample time and support to the best available linguists, well versed in the subjects concerned as well as in the languages from which, and into which, the translation is to be made. Some ancient Oriental writings on aesthetics read fairly simply and clearly; others, especially in literary Chinese, are full of obscure metaphors and allusions to other ancient writing. For these no bare translation, however correct in a literal way, can suffice. The common reader is helpless without a fringe of footnotes to explain, in part, the associations which each term conveyed in the original

4

tongue and cultural environment. When experts disagree on a certain rendering, as they often do, the layman is doubly helpless. He must, in principle, approve the zeal for perfection which impels some experts to criticize each others' translations with devastating severity. But life is short, and sometimes a translation with a few minor errors is better than no translation at all. Too often the perfectionists confine themselves to linguistic minutiae, leaving the great works untranslated.

Aesthetics in both East and West concerns itself with all the arts in relation to each other and to culture as a whole. From this standpoint, it is unfortunate that the specialization of scholarship in both hemispheres makes it so difficult to assemble and correlate theoretical texts on all the Asiatic arts, old and new. In East and West, a large share of humanistic scholarship is focused on some one art, language, region, period, and topic. An expert on ancient Chinese literature may pay no attention to current research on Chinese visual art, and vice versa. Specialists in obscure fields like that of ancient Chinese music, where most of the original data are lost, disagree widely.

This book is not intended for advanced Orientalists.[1] It is intended for the general reader, and especially for students of art and aesthetics in the West who have not yet looked to the East for light on their problems. However, since it covers so large a field, specialists in any one language and culture may find something of value in the materials drawn from other areas. While so few of the original texts are available in translation, anyone who tries to study the whole field of Far Eastern aesthetics must rely to a large extent on secondary sources: on historical and interpretive accounts by modern authorities. Where these disagree or leave

[1] Specialists in Indian art are asked to excuse the omission of diacritical marks.

5

huge gaps in our knowledge, he can perform a service by restating the problem and calling for more light upon it. He may also hope to stimulate more interest in the subject among younger scholars by offering them a first, brief glimpse of a vast, important, little-known domain. In the meantime, scholars East and West are meeting, reading each others' books, and exchanging ideas. The time seems ripe for a more systematic introduction.

Well-chosen anthologies of excerpts from long, important works are a great help to the layman. They are often tantalizing, and specialists usually find them unsatisfactory. But for someone who wishes to skim off the main ideas from a long, miscellaneous list of rare books they are indispensable. For an introductory study of Oriental aesthetics, one can find some excellent translations with interpretive notes in recent anthologies.[2]

2. The growth of interest in Oriental art and aesthetics

Aesthetics has never become a fully international subject like the older sciences, through basing its generalizations on world-wide phenomena. As a Western subject, a branch of philosophy, it has long been based on a small selection of the arts and ideas of Greece, Rome, and a few other Western nations. At the same time, it has undertaken to generalize

[2] Especially the following, edited by Prof. W. T. de Bary and published by Columbia University: *Sources of Indian Tradition* (New York, 1958); *Sources of Chinese Tradition* (New York, 1960); *Sources of Japanese Tradition* (New York, 1958). See also Donald Keene (ed.), *Anthology of Japanese Literature* (New York, 1955) and Wing-tsit Chan, *A Source Book in Chinese Philosophy* (Princeton Univ. Press, 1963). A useful general bibliography with critical notes is Charles O. Hucker's *China: a Critical Bibliography* (Tucson, Univ. of Arizona Press, 1962).

about *all* art, *all* aesthetic experience, *all* the values of art in human society.

Hegel was the first Western writer to include an account of Oriental art in a philosophic history of world civilization. That account was ill-informed and lacking in appreciation. It could hardly have been otherwise in Europe at the time in which he wrote.

The neglect of Oriental ideas by Western aesthetics can no longer be attributed to any scarcity of good Oriental art in the West. It is not due to lack of good histories and critical interpretations of particular arts. The neglect is rather due, I believe, to the inertia of tradition in Western aesthetics itself; to its over-reliance on deduction from metaphysical assumptions about beauty or on highly specialized linguistic analysis. Too many of us in this field have assumed that all our problems could be adequately handled without reference to world art, or indeed to any art at all. Consequently we have not developed a broadly empirical approach with due attention to the great diversity of styles and values in the arts of different peoples and periods. We still tend to lean too heavily on basic concepts derived from such fragmentary knowledge of Western art as one could acquire in the eighteenth and early nineteenth centuries. However, the understanding of art history as a part of world-wide cultural evolution is gradually penetrating the backward subject of aesthetics in both East and West. The traditional isolationism of aesthetics is becoming harder to maintain. Since we have imported Eastern art with admiration and subjected it to historical study on a high level of connoisseurship, the next step is to examine the principles which influenced its production and criticism.

If Western aestheticians wish to go on ignoring Oriental art and theory, they might more accurately entitle their books "Western Aesthetics," instead of seeming to make false claims to universal scope. Important works on Oriental theories of art, both translations of classics and contemporary studies, are now appearing in English and other European languages. It seems to me that, henceforth, no general history of aesthetics on either side of the world should limit itself to ideas originating in its own hemisphere.

The only available histories of aesthetics in English at present make practically no reference to Oriental art or ideas.[3] Of the two recent, posthumous books in French by Raymond Bayer of the Sorbonne (Paris, 1961), the one entitled *Histoire de l'esthétique* treats it as a purely Western subject. The other, *L'Esthétique mondiale au XX⁰ siècle*, has brief notes on some recent writers in India, China, and Japan. The title indicates the author's awareness of the need for a world-wide approach to the subject.

The arts of the Far East are, of course, no novelty in the West. There was commerce between Han China and the Roman Empire, and since Marco Polo cultural interchange between East and West has grown to vast proportions. Works of Far Eastern art have been pouring into Western collections increasingly since the Renaissance. A fusion of rococo and some elements in Chinese decorative style produced the graceful hybrid known as *Chinoiserie*. Chinese and Japanese garden and flower arts have long been admired and emulated in the West. Oriental music influenced Debussy. Artistic diffusion in both directions has gone on at a rapid rate for over two centuries. Japanese prints have ap-

[3] These are: B. Bosanquet, *History of Aesthetics* (London, 1892); K. Gilbert and H. Kuhn, *A History of Esthetic* (Bloomington, Ind., 1953); Listowel, Earl of, *A Critical History of Modern Aesthetics* (London, 1933). An earlier history by William Knight, *The Philosophy of the Beautiful* (New York, 1891) includes a brief and wholly inadequate remark on "Asiatic Aesthetics." Quoting Max Müller, it says, "there is scarcely a trace of feeling for the Beautiful in the Brahminical or Buddhist writings." (p. 17).

8

pealed to a large public in the West, and have also influenced such leading artists as Manet, Degas, and van Gogh.

Along with importation of exotic art comes the need for authoritative interpretations of it. Many capable books on a semi-popular level have helped the West to appreciate Far Eastern art. Of this kind are the excellent, illustrated brochures published by the Japanese Board of Tourist Industry. In a simple, untechnical way, Lin Yu-tang has helped many Occidentals to like and understand the traditional Chinese way of life and some of its values.[4] Okakura-Kakuzo's *The Book of Tea* is a sympathetic introduction to Japanese culture. M. Anesaki's *Art, Life, and Nature in Japan* and Jiro Harada's *A Glimpse of Japanese Ideals* were addressed to an educated, general public and contained much theory in simple wording. Histories and interpretations of particular arts of the Far East have been written by experts from both sides of the world during the late nineteenth and early twentieth centuries.[5] Expert translators such as Arthur Waley and Donald Keene have brought us some of the cream of Chinese and Japanese literature in

[4] E.g., in *My Country and My People* (New York, 1936).

[5] For example, the following: E. F. Fenollosa, *Epochs of Chinese and Japanese Art* (New York, 1921); R. Petrucci, "Morceaux choisis d'Esthétique" (*Ostasiatische Zeitschrift*, vol. I, no. 1, Jan. 1915); K. Glaser, *Ostasiatische Plastik* (Berlin, 1925) and others in the series *Die Kunst des Ostens*, edited by W. Cohn; H. A. Giles, Introduction to the *History of Chinese Pictorial Art* (London, 1918); O. Sirèn, *A History of Early Chinese Painting* (London, 1933); *Gardens of China* (New York, 1949); T. Tamura, *Art of the Landscape Garden in Japan* (New York, 1936); A. Waley, *Introduction to the Study of Chinese Painting* (London, 1923); R. Grousset, *Civilization of the East: India; China; Japan* (New York, 1934); G. S. de Morant, *History of Chinese Art* (London, n.d.); N. Minamoto, *An Illustrated History of Japanese Art* (Kyoto, 1935); A. R. Coomaraswamy, *Introduction to Indian Art* (Madras, 1923); S. Kramrisch, *Indian Sculpture* (London, 1933); H. Zimmer, *Myths and Symbols in Indian Art and Civilization* (New York, 1946).

9

verse and prose, with explanatory notes. Our museums are richly endowed with works of Oriental visual art in many media, ancient and modern. We now have films and phonograph records of Oriental music, dance, and theater. Capable historians and museum officials are helping to organize these materials chronologically and relate them to their cultural settings. Experts in specialized fields such as Sung porcelain and Rajput miniatures, Japanese screens and music, Noh plays and Kabuki, have shown the public how to recognize historic styles and distinctive features in these typical Eastern media. They have shown us how the Oriental connoisseur regards and judges the art of his own country: for example, the emphasis placed on slight nuances of brush-stroke, characteristic of an individual artist, rather than on the more obvious features of design, composition, and representation which tend to impress the Western observer more at first sight.

All these activities offer materials for aesthetics but do not in themselves constitute a fully organized subject of aesthetics. Insofar as they contain some general, theoretical discussion, they overlap the field of aesthetics, but books of history organize their materials in a mainly chronological sequence, and do not often discuss broad theoretical problems at length.

Aesthetics was formerly defined in the West as a branch of philosophy dealing with beauty. It is coming to be understood as a semi-independent subject, on its way toward scientific status; as devoted to the theoretical study of the arts and related types of behavior and experience. In trying to understand these phenomena, it seeks new information from other branches of scholarship, especially art criticism, psychology, sociology, anthropology, art history, and cultural history. Aesthetics tends to organize its materials in logical or theoretical order, as generalizations on the varieties of art and related kinds of human activity in a social context.

3. Possible values for Western aesthetics in Oriental writings on related subjects

What values can the Western aesthetician hope to find in traditional Far Eastern theories of art? Three kinds of value, I believe.

One is that of adding to our knowledge of the history of ideas, and hence of general cultural history. As written by some Western historians these subjects, like aesthetics itself, are heavily over-balanced on the Western side, as if the development of thought had followed only one sequence from Egypt and Greece to modern Europe. But it has long been recognized that, from the earliest historic times, Oriental philosophers, rulers, priests, and diviners were meditating on problems much like those which challenged Western minds. Indian and Chinese sages were meditating on the arts and their potential values for man about the same time that Pythagoras, Plato, and Aristotle were doing so in the West. Later Indian aesthetics is in some ways analogous to medieval European aesthetics. A comparison of Eastern and Western thought shows many surprising resemblances. Similar theories arose at about the same time in widely separate parts of the earth.

How to explain them is a major problem of cultural history. In general, the only two ways of doing so are (a) independent invention and (b) diffusion or influence of one culture on another. No doubt there has been some of both. We do not know how much cultural interchange there was between East and West in ancient times, but certainly there has been an increasing amount in recent centuries, includ-

11

ing works of art and ideas about them. Cultural relations between East and West have long been a two-way traffic.

A second type of value which the West can hope to find in Oriental aesthetic theories is help in understanding Oriental art; especially the styles of art which come from the same environment. On the whole, the styles and trends in art usually came first, perhaps antedating by centuries the attempts to evaluate them in a very general way and to formulate rules of art on that basis. But the principles laid down by respected authorities, such as Aristotle in the West, Lu Chi and Bharata in the East, could strongly reinforce one kind of art and discourage others. The influence between art and aesthetics was sometimes strong in both directions. At other times (as today in Europe) aesthetics has comparatively little influence on art; it lags far behind in adjusting its conceptions of what art is and ought to be to the changed realities of art itself. But at any time and place, the relations between the arts and contemporary theories of art are significant for an understanding of both, and of the culture in which both operate.

Many of the classical Eastern writings on theory are by noted artists, referring explicitly to their own works and those of other individuals. Whether or not the particular works referred to are still extant, the comments may imply influential current attitudes. Often they suggest symbolic and metaphorical meanings which a literal, superficial view of the work would not reveal.

The Occidental scholar has every right to retain his own ways of looking at art; his own tastes and standards for judging it, whatever its origin. But he may also wish, at times, to look at it from the standpoint of its cultural context. No one from a distant culture can do this completely. We have our habits and attitudes, from which we cannot escape entirely, even if we so desire. But it is possible to do so in some degree. Studying the total culture-pattern and psychological climate of an epoch, especially its attitudes toward the kind of art in question, can help us respond to particular works in a more understanding, sympathetic way.

A third type of possible value is that of increasing our understanding of art in general, including our own contemporary arts. The revision is likely to be in the direction of greater breadth and catholicity. More experience of world art in its infinite variety, and more understanding of the reasons why people of different cultures have made, used, enjoyed, and criticized it as they have, tend to make one's standards more relative and more pluralistic. It becomes harder and harder to cling to a few simple, absolute rules, based on a narrow sampling of European arts and ideas. As we have come to recognize that Oriental art contains important values not attained by art in the West, so we may discover important insights in Oriental aesthetics, applicable to art and aesthetic experience everywhere. Many Western artists and critics believe that our art has much to learn from Eastern methods. This is controversial, but certainly Western art has learned from Eastern art and philosophy in the past and may do so again.

Aesthetics is not yet fully and consistently scientific anywhere in the world. It will not become so in the near future, if ever. It is now less purely philosophical and normative than it used to be; more descriptive and empirical. Judging by the contents of its periodicals and the programs of its conventions, it is usually a mixture of many different approaches, expressing the viewpoints of scholars in various fields who share a common interest in the theoretical understanding of the arts. Some books and articles, classed under the heading of aesthetics, are mainly literary in tone; a sort of generalized art criticism. Some are mainly historical; perhaps as histories of a concept such as beauty or of a style such as the baroque. Some deal with basic philosophical issues such as value in art; some report psychological, anthropological, or sociological researches bearing on the arts. Few published works combine all these different points of view. However, something is accomplished by bringing them together in a convention program or between the covers of a magazine. This at least helps the reader to interrelate them for himself. That has long been the policy of the leading periodicals on aesthetics in Europe and North America.

4. Aesthetics in Japan and India today

Apparently it is also the policy of the excellent Japanese quarterly on aesthetics, *Bigaku*.[6] Not reading Japanese, I can judge only from the tables of contents and summaries of articles which it prints in each issue in English or some other Western language. (These are, of course, indispensable to readers who do not know Japanese. They set a good example to other periodicals. Most magazines in English are remiss in this respect.) Looking again through my file of issues up to the present, I have confirmed my high opinion of its level of scholarship, independent thinking, and international scope. All the main viewpoints mentioned above are represented. Attention is given to a wide variety of arts and ideas about them—some Oriental, some Occidental; some traditional, some contemporary. In art and aesthetics, as in other fields, the Japanese have persistently reached out to all parts of the world for modern ideas, methods, and subjects of study which promise to be valuable. At the same time, they do not neglect their own heritage. Traditional Japanese arts are actively preserved and

[6] It started in 1950 and is published by the Japanese Society for Aesthetics, in care of the Faculty of Letters, Tokyo University, in collaboration with Bijutsu Shuppan-sha.

14

cultivated in modern Japan. New, vigorous styles are appearing, some Oriental in spirit and some constructively eclectic.

In the summaries of articles in *Bigaku*, I notice a prevailing tone of objective, empirical, clear-headed scholarship. Important foreign books are reviewed at length. The influence of German philosophy is still surprisingly strong, in view of the fact that Germany has done little in aesthetics since the Second World War, and that German philosophic idealism has lost much of its former prestige. Is this survival due in part to old political, military, and educational ties?

Among Asiatic nations now on friendly terms with the West, Japan is by far the most active in aesthetics on an organized, professional basis. It has a vigorous society for aesthetics with regular meetings and sends representatives to the international congresses. The chief obstacle to better communication between Japanese and Western aestheticians is linguistic and geographical, not religious or ideological. It could be overcome by more translations, and one can hardly imagine a better step toward international aesthetics than publication in English or French of the complete files of *Bigaku*.

There seems to be a scarcity in Japan of large, comprehensive, systematic books on general aesthetics. A few of these by leading authorities would help to bring together some of the ideas which are now scattered in many short articles and books of essays. Even on the textbook level, they would serve to organize the subject and perhaps express a national point of view. This need is not filled by the many specialized books on Japanese art.[7]

[7] A book of Japanese essays on the arts was recently edited by Isaku Yanaihara under the title, *Nihon Shisō taikei* (*The Grand Collection of Contemporary Japanese Thoughts*). Publisher: Chikuma

In India, English is not only well established as a second language, but is often used in preference to any native language for official and scholarly communication. It is known to many educated people throughout India and Pakistan. Several important long, systematic books on aesthetics have recently been published in English by Indian scholars. On the other hand, one hears of no steps toward a professional organization or periodical in aesthetics there. One small magazine on the subject was started a few years ago, but soon expired. (I am not thinking now of magazines on philosophy or on art, such as *Marg*, which occasionally print articles on aesthetics.)

Many Indian scholars do not seem as receptive to Western ideas on art, aesthetics, and the humanities as the Japanese are. It is still a common view in India that its own culture is far superior to the West in "spiritual values," and that India can learn from the West only practical, materialistic subjects like engineering, sanitation, and mass production. This prejudice is, I think, being outgrown by the younger generation of Indian scholars; at least by those who have traveled and studied more in the West.

I have not been able to find in either India, Japan, or China any single treatise on aesthetics, old or new, which covers the basic problems common to *all* the arts. At the most, one finds a single combined art such as drama and theater, discussed with broad implications for art in general. The lack of such a comprehensive treatise is partly explained by the recent origin of the concepts of "art" and "aesthetics" in the modern senses of these terms. The term "art," as restricted to aesthetic skills and products and excluding the mainly utilitarian ones such as medicine, war, and mining, did not come into general use in the West

Shobo, Tokyo, August 1964. It will be translated by Makoto Ueda, who kindly supplied this reference.

until the eighteenth century. "Aesthetics" as a name for the philosophy of art and beauty is largely a nineteenth-century Hegelian invention. Both terms are still very ambiguous. The fields they designate are vaguely defined, and scholars do not agree as to how to organize research and writing in them. Aesthetics is far from being accepted as a major, necessary branch of philosophy, East or West. I have found little or no mention of aesthetics, art, beauty, and related terms in most of the histories of Asiatic philosophy.[8]

5. Native and foreign traditions in twentieth-century Chinese aesthetics

In Communist China, a strong effort is being made to destroy or weaken the influence of old traditions on modern intellectual life. Some points of resemblance between Confucian and Communist collectivism have been carefully publicized. Old ideas not too hostile to the régime are salvaged here and there, along with traditional works of art, to preserve what is now regarded as the best in China's heritage. These are reinterpreted in accord with the new dogma, to provide a partial synthesis. In aesthetics the native Confucian, Taoist, and Buddhist traditions have been largely replaced by the Marxist one, imported from the West. (Buddhism is, of course, not a strictly native tradition, but has for centuries been domesticated in accord with the Chinese environment.) Marxist aesthetics has been restated by Mao Tse-Tung and others with a strongly partisan, socioeconomic, and political emphasis.[9]

[8] E.g., S. Dasgupta's *History of Indian Philosophy*, 5 vols. (Cambridge Univ. Press, 1932–55); Fung Yu-lan, *History of Chinese Philosophy*, 2 vols. (Peiping, Vetch, 1937, and Princeton Univ. Press, 1 vol., 1953). The shorter version of Dr. Fung's book has a little on aesthetics.

[9] Some of these statements have been published in English by the

17

The Marxist theory claims to be scientific and is so in some respects, but it lacks the freedom of discussion, research, experiment, and publication which is characteristic of a true science in the liberal world. As in the U.S.S.R., aesthetics as a field of intellectual activity is taken more seriously by the Chinese government than it usually is in the West. This is because it is regarded, not as a field of ineffectual speculation about beauty, but as concerned with the practical uses of art for strengthening the Communist régime and culture. A good deal of competent work in archeology and art history is now being done in Communist China. This is partly because it is more possible in those fields to avoid controversial issues and imposed party lines of thought. Communist and non-Communist ideas on aesthetics come quickly into conflict, although they do not disagree completely. Chinese newspapers and magazines now publish a good deal of theoretical discussion of the arts, and there seems to be a lively popular interest in it.

Lip service has been paid in Chinese official directives to the liberal ideals of encouraging creative originality and variety of style, form, genre, and subject-matter in the arts. There is talk of cherishing the best in the cultural heritage of Eastern and Western art and criticism. Mao Tse-Tung's

Foreign Language Press: for example, Mao Tse-Tung, *Talks at the Yenan Forum on Art and Literature* (Peking, 1956, 1960); *On Art and Literature* (Peking, 1960); Chou Yang, *The Path of Socialist Literature and Art in China* (Peking, 1960). This last was a report delivered to the Third Congress of Chinese Literary and Art Workers in July, 1960. A multigraphed set of translations, entitled *Some Articles in the Communist Chinese Press on the 20th Anniversary of Publication of Mao Tse-Tung's Talks at Yenan Forum on Literature and Art*, was issued by the American Consulate General in Hong Kong on July 3, 1962 (No. 685). It includes comments on many particular works of art. On Marxist aesthetics in general, see T. Munro, "The Marxist Theory of Art History: Socio-economic Determinism and the Dialectical Process," *Journal of Aesthetics and Art Criticism*, XVIII, 4 (June 1960), pp. 430–445; with bibliography.

apparently liberal slogan, "Let a hundred flowers blossom, let a hundred schools of thought contend," was enthusiastically applied to the arts for a brief interval. But the reaction soon appeared in a call to root out "poisonous weeds" and maintain "a critical attitude toward the cultural heritage." "That literature and art must serve the broad masses of laboring people and the great cause of socialism and communism is the sole political line for the literature and art of our country." [10]

Fortunately for our knowledge of traditional Chinese theories of art, many non-Communist scholars now live outside the mainland. Some important manuscripts and early printed books are also in free hands, and several of these on art and aesthetics have been translated into European languages in recent years.

A valuable short book by a French Jesuit, Father O. Brière, was put into English by L. G. Thompson and published in 1956 as *Fifty Years of Chinese Philosophy* (1898–1950).[11] It is divided into three sections: (I) "The Movement of Ideas from 1898 to 1950," including those of Darwin, Spencer, Kropotkin, Nietzsche, Marx, Dewey, and Russell in addition to Confucianism and Buddhism; (II) "The Systems of Oriental Derivation," mostly idealistic or vitalistic, and (III) "The Systems of Occidental Derivation," some based on Western science, some on Marxism and some otherwise materialistic. A long bibliography in English and Chinese follows.

Aesthetics figures occasionally in both the traditional and foreign ideas discussed. Ts'ai Yüan-p'ei is cited as an advocate of "aestheticism." A progressive Confucianist and Minister of Education, he had studied aesthetics at Leipzig and later proposed that art be made a substitute for religion as a

---

[10] Chou Yang, *op. cit.*, pp. 20f, 30f.
[11] (London, G. Allen and Unwin, 1956).

source of beauty and consolation. This is based on an old Chinese tradition, Father Brière notes (pp. 31–2). Fu T'ung-hsien, idealist and professor of philosophy in Shanghai, expressed his Hegelian views in an *Outline of Aesthetics* (1948). During the thirties and forties Chu Kuang-ch'ien published a series of books on aesthetics from the idealistic standpoint of Benedetto Croce: *The Psychology of Literary Art* (1936), *On Beauty* (1932), and *On Poetry* (1948). "The highest form of practical morals," he said, "is artistic activity, since the summit of supreme good and absolute beauty coincide."

Before the Communist rule prevailed, several scholars preached liberal, non-Marxist varieties of Western materialism and positivism (pp. 84–5). Few of these dealt with aesthetics. Hu Shih, a follower of Deweyan pragmatism, sought to Westernize Chinese culture in many respects; also to encourage the native tradition of realistic, popular fiction, informal in style and language.

Hu Shih became a diplomat and administrator, staying away from the mainland most of his time. Except for him and his associates, it would seem that the main conflict in aesthetics during these pre-Communist years was that between German-Italian idealism and Marxist materialism. Liberal Western naturalism, empiricism, and pragmatism did not make themselves very strongly felt in this realm of thought. During the period of struggle before the Communist take-over, the Confucianist, Taoist, and Buddhist traditions were rapidly losing influence in academic and artistic circles.

After the Communist victory, Ts'ai undertook a Marxist theoretical study of art and aesthetics, including *The New Aesthetics* (1948) and *The Sociology of Art*. Others of the same school translated Occidental works of art history and biography. One of these, Hu Man, wrote a *History of the*

Fine Arts in China (1942) with this admonition: "Art, in the past, was based on the exploitation of the people, the workers: It is now a question of restoring to the common masses their artistic heritage." (p. 98).

6. Some comparisons between Chinese and Western theories of music, fiction, and drama

Both Plato and Confucius thought of music as a means of producing the right kinds of emotion, attitude, and character; hence as means to strengthening the state. Music was to be stately and dignified, simpler than the popular music of the time. It should be such as to develop attitudes of inner harmony, joy, and peace; also powers of rational self-control in the individual, especially those entrusted with government. "Let a man be first incited by the *Songs*," Confucius taught, "then given a firm footing by the study of ritual and finally perfected by music." [12] Confucius did not emphasize the need for maintaining primitive simplicity in music as much as Plato did. (*Analects* III: 23; *cf*. Plato, *Laws*). He preferred peaceful to warlike beauty in the dance, and did not emphasize the martial aspects of education. (III: 25).

Hsün Tzu, Confucian scholar of the Chou dynasty, declared that "The former kings set up rites and music that men might be controlled by them." Great music must be easy, great rites simple. "Music induces an end to anger; music is the harmony of heaven and earth. Through harmony all things are transformed." Not only does the right kind of music benefit the state, but also a well-ruled state expresses itself in joyous, peaceful music. "That of a country

[12] *Analects*, A. Waley (trans.), VII: 8; also XVII: 9. (London, B. Watson (tr.), *Haün Tzu, Mo Tzu* (Columbia, 1963).

21

in confusion is full of resentment and anger and its government is disordered; that of a dying country is mournful and pensive and its people are in distress. The ways of music and of government are thus directly related." [13]

One thinks of Plato also in reading that the "heavenly patterns" are to serve as models for human behavior and for literary forms and ideas.[14] On the other hand, one is closer to Epicurus and Greek hedonism in reading the Taoist Yang Chu in the *Lieh Tzu:* "Then what is the purpose of life? What is the joy of life? Life is only for the enjoyment of beauty and wealth, and sound and color." [15]

As early as 239 B.C., it is said, a method was invented in China for deriving the standard musical tones arithmetically from a fundamental pitch-pipe. (Compare the Pythagorean discoveries of the mathematical and physical basis of pitch in the lyre.) Such orderly production of sounds was related to order in the universe, including the cycle of the seasons. Absolute pitch was maintained by standard pitch-pipes of uniform length and capacity. Belief in the magical power of sounds and numbers (again a Pythagorean idea) was extended to a belief in the power of music to maintain or destroy the harmony of the universe. Hence the first duty

[13] *Sources of Chinese Tradition*, pp. 183f, quoting the *Li Chi*, §19. Cf. Fung Yu-lan, *A Short History of Chinese Philosophy* (New York, Macmillan, 1948), p. 150. Wing-tsit Chan (*op. cit.*, p. 18) lists Confucian references to the arts. He quotes Chou Tun-I, a Neo-Confucianist (1017–1073), as praising ancient music. In a treatise on the Book of Changes, Chou described it as calm, harmonious, and moderate. Modern music, he said, is "seductive, licentious, depressive, and complaining. It arouses desires and increases bitterness without end." (*Source Book*, pp. 472f). See also Siu-chi Huang, "Musical Art in Early Confucian Philosophy," *Philosophy East and West*, XIII, 1 (April 1963), pp. 49–59.

[14] Liu Hsieh, *The Literary Mind and the Carving of Dragons*, pp. 8–13.

[15] *Sources of Chinese Tradition*, p. 291.

22

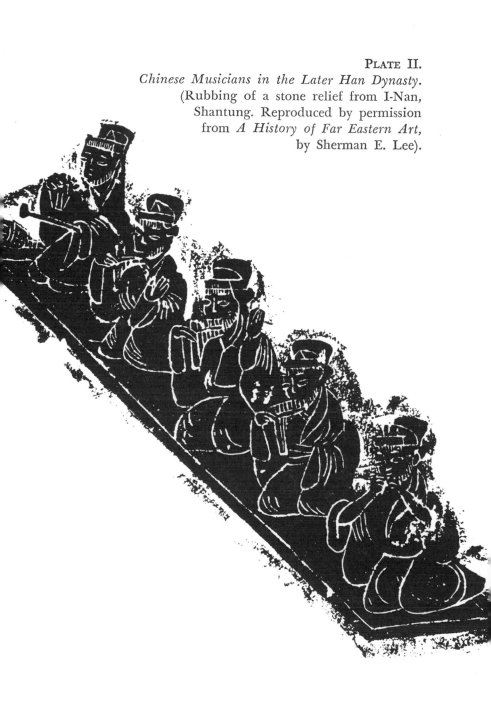

PLATE II.
Chinese Musicians in the Later Han Dynasty.
(Rubbing of a stone relief from I-Nan,
Shantung. Reproduced by permission
from *A History of Far Eastern Art,*
by Sherman E. Lee).

PLATE III. *A Chinese Gentleman Enjoying the Art of Paintin*
Panel from a Japanese screen representing "The Four Eleg
Accomplishments." Attributed to Kanō Takanobu, 1511–16
(Courtesy of The Seattle Art Museu

of a ruler was to maintain tradition in music and ritual.[16] Music for universal harmony suggests the Pythagorean, Platonic, and medieval belief in the music of the heavenly spheres.[17] Antoine Meillet remarks that the similarity between ancient Greek and Indian music is too exact and manifold to be due to chance.[18] P. J. Chaudhury finds a detailed analogy between Aristotle's theory of catharsis and the psychotherapeutic function of drama as set forth by Bharata and his followers in India.[19]

[16] E. Wellesz (ed.), *Ancient and Oriental Music* (London, 1957). This contains a chapter on ancient Chinese music by L. Picken, with bibliography. On various aspects of Chinese music, see also C. Sachs, *The Rise of Music in the Ancient World, East and West* (New York, 1943), Section Three on East Asia. These two books contain extensive bibliographies: Chao-Mei-Pa, *The Yellow Bell* (Baldwin, Md., Bayberry Mill, 1934) and J. H. Levis, *Foundations of Chinese Musical Art* (Peiping, Vetch, 1936). A third-century prose poem on the history and theory of instrumental music was translated with notes by R. H. Van Gulick under the title, *Hsi K'ang and his Poetical Essay on the Lute* (Tokyo, Sophia Univ., 1941). A new edition has recently appeared of *The Prose Poetry of Su Tung P'o*, who lived in the eleventh century. (New York, Paragon, 1964). Translated by C. D. L. Clark, it has an introduction on the poet's philosophy of art, especially music and painting. This combined Confucianist, Buddhist, and Taoist influences. A translator's note states that the music which pleased Confucius was destroyed in 213 B.C. and replaced by a kind introduced from Bactria in the second century B.C., with Greek influence. (p. 58). A *fu* or prose poem by Su Tung P'o on "Modern Music in the Yen Ho Palace" is included in this volume, pp. 55–69. It tells of efforts to maintain a standard, uniform pitch.

[17] Denied by Aristotle, Albertus, and St. Thomas, this idea was revived by Dante (*Paradiso*, I, 76). Cf. Karl Vossler, *Medieval Culture*, I, 141.

[18] Wellesz, p. 196.

[19] "Catharsis in the Light of Indian Aesthetics," *Journal of Aesthetics and Art Criticism*, XV, 2 (Dec. 1956), p. 215, referring to R. K. Sen, *A Comparative Study of Greek and Indian Poetics and Aesthetics* (Calcutta, 1954).

Plato's attitude toward music was ultra-conservative in calling for a return to ancient simplicity and for a council of elders to regulate the arts. Likewise Neo-Confucianism called for a conservative attitude with admiration and emulation of the ancient classics. This was common among Confucian scholars in China up to recent times. It was echoed by the Confucian Japanese writer Fujiwara no Teika (c. 1200), who insisted on close imitation of classical sentiments and expressions.[20] In the Western Renaissance likewise, a spirit of veneration for the Greek and Roman classics arose which lasted well on into the eighteenth century. In both East and West, this included a disparaging attitude toward contemporary art, which was long assumed to be in a state of decline.[21]

Both Platonists and Confucianists regarded the ancient arts of music, poetry, and ritual as desirable means of educating future officials of the state: not so much for any specific information or skill to be learned (indeed, the performance of art was often thought to be beneath the dignity of a ruler) as for the type of character and attitude to be developed. In China, ability to understand and practice certain classical rules of literary composition was a qualification for high political rank as determined by the imperial examination system, especially in and after the T'ang dynasty. There were also official examinations in the art of painting. The imperial examinations served as tests of moral character, intelligence, industry, and learning ability, which were thought to be transferable to public affairs and doubtless were to some extent. Both Platonists and Confucianists thought of the ideal educational system as one

[20] *Sources of Japanese Tradition*, p. 183.
[21] *Cf.* Liu Hsieh, *The Literary Mind and the Carving of Dragons*, p. 4.

24

which opened the door to high rank through innate individual ability and education, rather than hereditary rank alone. In theory at least, a Chinese boy without hereditary rank or wealth could, by mental aptitude and education, rise to power in the state or to a position of respect as an artist or scholar.[22] In practice, the very poor and humble were not likely to have much opportunity for education. In a large empire, standardized examinations were more appropriate than in the small, ideal city-state which Plato envisaged. In both cultures, respect for mental ability was coupled with conservatism in the classical periods, including a tendency to perpetuate the hierarchy of social classes.

Some of the early Chinese sages took a negative view toward art, as useless or involving too much planful effort to improve things. Mo Tzu said, "To engage in music is wrong." If useless, this and other fine arts were to be eliminated.[23] But later Taoism became a prolific inspiration to Chinese and Japanese art, in alliance with Ch'an-Zen Buddhism. It developed a host of deities and minor spirits, all potential subjects for the artist; also, it was more free and individualistic, less devoted to past rules and classics. The Taoist veneration of nature, as imbued with a spirit which

[22] On this question see Ping-ti Ho, *The Ladder of Success in Imperial China: Aspects of Social Mobility, 1368–1911* (New York, Columbia Univ. Press, 1962).

[23] See Y. L. Fung (Fung Yu-lan), *History of Chinese Philosophy* (Peiping, Vetch, 1937), vol. I, p. 90. Music is bad, according to Mo Tzu, because it wastes time and the people's resources and causes people to neglect their work. (See Wing-tsit Chan, *Source Book in Chinese Philosophy*, pp. 227). Said Lao Tzu: "The five colors blind the eye. The five tones deafen the ear. The five flavors cloy the palate. Racing and hunting madden the mind. Rare goods tempt men to do wrong." *Tao Teh Ching*, tr. by J. C. H. Wu (New York, St. John's Univ. Press, 1961), p. 15. Early Chinese attitudes toward music are further explained by Siu-chi Huang in "Musical Art in Early Confucian Philosophy." *Philosophy East and West*, XIII, No. 1 (Apr. 1963), pp. 49–59.

could join the human observer with hills and streams, was more akin to Western romanticism than to either Plato or Aristotle.[24]

There are many other analogies between East and West in the history of the arts and in that of philosophic ideals regarding their social functions. Such terms as "geometric," "archaic," "classic," "baroque," "rococo," and "romantic" are applied to certain styles in both East and West, regarded as significantly similar. Some historians hold that these recurrent types appear in about the same sequence in Eastern and Western civilization, but this remains to be proved.

The art of the novel reached high peaks of development in Europe and in China in the late seventeenth and eighteenth centuries, but no influence in either direction can be found which is sufficient to explain this parallelism. The presence of a few Jesuit priests in China is not enough to explain a novel as mature in psychological realism and as complex in structure as the *Chin P'ing Mei*. For the *Tale of Genji* (early eleventh century) there is no contemporary parallel in the West.[25] To explain such analogies is a persistent problem in cultural history.[26] In many cases there

---

[24] *Cf. Sources of Chinese Tradition*, pp. 291ff. Taoist influence appears in the poetical comments of T'ao Ch'ien (4th–5th century). James R. Hightower has translated and annotated three of his prose poems in "The *Fu* of T'ao Ch'ien," *Harvard Journal of Asiatic Studies*, XVII (1954), 169–230. See also W. R. B. Acker (trans.), *T'ao the Hermit: Sixty Poems by T'ao Ch'ien* (London, Thames and Hudson, 1952); Chang Chung-yuan, *Creativity and Taoism; a Study of Chinese Philosophy, Art, and Poetry* (New York, Julian Press, 1963).

[25] C. P. Fitzgerald's *China: a Short Cultural History* (New York, 1958) has a good chapter on the novel, pp. 500ff, as well as on art and theories of art in the principal dynasties.

[26] See A. L. Kroeber, *Configurations of Culture Growth* (Berkeley, Calif., 1944), esp. on the novel. Also his *The Nature of Culture* (Univ. of Chicago Press, 1952), pp. 409ff on "The Novel in Asia and Europe." *Cf.* R. G. Irwin, *The Evolution of a Chinese Novel* (Cambridge, Mass., Harvard Univ. Press, 1953). A pioneer work on the Chinese novel was

seems to have been no possibility of influence from one region to another; yet historians hesitate to rely too much on parallelism or independent invention. In later periods, influence in one or both directions is more probable.

Chinese officials and influential scholars, trained in the austere traditions of Confucianism and Buddhism, disapproved of the novel and of many shorter tales which preceded it. To them it represented the sort of popular, undisciplined, highly colored, often indecent and exciting entertainment which Plato excluded from his ideal state. Popular fiction is rather ignored than explicitly denounced in the classical writings on aesthetics which are now available to foreign scholars. We know that it was considered disreputable and sometimes dangerous for a scholar or gentleman to acknowledge authorship of such fiction and that many widely read novels are anonymous or attributed to pseudonyms. Corrupt and incompetent scholar-bureaucrats of the traditional Confucianist type were satirized in the Ch'ing dynasty novel, *The Scholars*.[27]

Much is to be learned about classical Chinese attitudes toward the drama. Henry H. Hart, in an introduction to his translation of *The West Chamber: a Medieval Drama*,[28]

---

published in pamphlet form by Pearl Buck under the title, *East and West and the Novel: Sources of the Early Chinese Novel* (Peiping, North China Union Language School, 1932). Mrs. Buck also translated the *Shui-hu chuan*, an early novel of the Robin Hood type, with the English title *All Men Are Brothers* (New York, Grove, 1957). This is one of the three novels which Mrs. Buck dated in the Yüan or early Ming period, and considers as marking the height of the Chinese novel. This view would be contested today by many who prefer the later ones, just mentioned.

[27] Trans. by H. and G. Yang (Peking, Foreign Languages Press, 1957).

[28] (Stanford, Calif., Stanford Univ. Press, 1936). The *Hsi-hsiang-chi*, a 13th-century drama. See also Sophia Delza, "The Classic Chinese Theater," *Journal of Aesthetics and Art Criticism*, XV 2 (Dec. 1956), pp. 181–197. Several other references are in Hucker, pp. 87ff.

briefly summarizes the history of the Chinese drama. Like that of Greece, he says, it had its roots in sacred rituals; in the Chou dynasty, six varieties of ceremonial dance were recognized. *The West Chamber*, though popular for centuries as one of the ten "works of genius," has been ignored by conservative scholars. "In spite of their passionate devotion to the theater," says Hart, "they have always held it and the acting profession in the utmost contempt... No scholar ever cared to write dramatic commentaries of criticism." The first serious studies along that line are fairly recent, such as the *History of the Drama during the Sung and Yüan Dynasties,* by Wang Kuo Wei. Without benefit of scholarly approval, the drama throve abundantly during the Yüan and Ming dynasties, evolving more and more complex forms as it did in Greece. (See Aristotle's account in the *Poetics*.)

On the Chinese theory of the drama, Hart comments that its name (*hsi*) in Chinese means literally "to mock, to make fun of, to ridicule, to satirize, to joke." Accordingly, the drama was regarded as mere play-acting, "not to be taken seriously as we take our drama." This in spite of the fact that it was usually made to preach an edifying moral lesson, even at the cost of artistic faults. "As in painting, sculpture, and other art expressions of the Chinese, the form is subservient to the ethical purpose." [29]

The low opinion held of the drama by many Chinese scholars is in marked contrast with the respect and emphasis given to this art by scholars and the public in India. It recalls Aristotle's cavalier treatment of comedy in the *Poetics*, as an art that "shows people as worse than they are." Chinese drama, Hart adds, was romantic rather than classic,

---

[29] P. xxv. This statement seems to me exaggerated. A great deal of Chinese art has no discernible moral purpose other than aesthetic enjoyment.

28

in allowing the artist to change time, place, and action-sequence freely.

7. Traditional Indian aesthetics in English

The most comprehensive publication by a single author on the combined field of Indian and Western aesthetics, as far as I know, is the monumental series of volumes by Professor K. C. Pandey of Lucknow University on *Comparative Aesthetics*.[30] Volume I, recently enlarged in a second edition, is on *Indian Aesthetics;* Volume II on *Western Aesthetics.* Dr. Pandey displays in Volume II a considerable knowledge of European philosophy from Plato through Croce, but limits his survey of Western aesthetics almost entirely to the idealistic tradition. This he compares with the Indian treatment of similar concepts. He is preparing a revised enlargement of the Western volume which promises to do more justice to other schools of Western thought.

The volume on Indian aesthetics, which will be of most interest to Western readers, contains a huge amount of valuable historical material, most of which is probably unfamiliar to all but a few Sanskrit specialists. It is clearly written in English, amply documented and annotated in both English and Sanskrit. It provides a detailed account of Indian aesthetics from Bharata's theory of drama (c. 500 A.D.) through the development of a philosophy of music some seven hundred years later. There is a section on the medieval philosophy of architecture and an intensive study of Abhinavagupta (c. 1000). This great aesthetician developed Bharata's theory of *rasa* and used it in explaining the techniques, forms, and values of drama, poetry, and other arts of the theater. There are many definitions of *rasa*, a key

---

[30] (Varanasi-I, India, Chowkhambra Sanskrit Series Office, 1956–59).

conception in Indian aesthetics, to which we shall return. Primarily, it means "flavor" (in food, art, or elsewhere); also the enjoyment of flavor. Dr. Pandey also translates it as "the object of relish" and (in a more introverted way) "the act of relishing." (p. 142).

The earliest Indian writings on art, Dr. Pandey explains, were mostly on technique; the later ones more philosophical and psychological. The history of Indian aesthetics is an integral part of the history of Indian philosophy and religion. Hence it is related to the systems of Vedanta and Samkhya, to Saivism, and to certain types of yoga. Abhinavagupta was "a rational mystic," Dr. Pandey declares, "because his philosophical ideas are based not only on supersensuous experience but also on reason." (p. 87). "His aesthetic theory is based on the Saiva metaphysics and epistemology." He was "an idealist in holding that reality is ideal and not sensuous . . . that thought and being are identical; that there is nothing apart from thought; thought is thing . . . The process of world-reason is identical with that of reason operative in the individual mind." [31]

A short but very concise essay by Professor Pandey, entitled "Indian Aesthetics," provides a good introduction to the whole subject.[32] Defining aesthetics as the science and philosophy of fine art, he shows that the different schools of philosophic thought in India explain aesthetic experience in different ways. Authorities on poetry, music, and architecture agree "that art presents the Absolute as conceived by them." Thus, from the start, we are in much the same

[31] Dr. Pandey has recently published a volume entirely devoted to this philosopher: *Abhinavagupta, an Historical and Philosophical Study* (Varanasi-I, India, Chowkhambra Sanskrit Series Office, 1963).

[32] In *History of Philosophy, Eastern and Western*, by S. Radhakrishnan and others (2 vols., London, G. Allen and Unwin, 1952), pp. 472ff. See also H. L. Sharma, "A Critical Survey of Indian Aesthetics," *Journal of the Jha Research Institute*, XVII, Pts. 1–4, 1961.

realm of idealistic metaphysics as that conceived by Plato, Plotinus, Kant, and Hegel, even though points of disagreement with all of these are mentioned. Aesthetics has been discussed in India "from the technical, metaphysical, psychological, epistemic, logical, and critical points of view"; also in regard to the end of art, the artist, and the aesthete or appreciator. *Rasa* is defined here (p. 474) as "what a dramatist presents"; "the object of aesthetic relish." It is a "unity in multiplicity" in which the unifying factor is a basic state of mind which binds together (1) the emotive situation in a human setting with a physical cause, (2) mimetic changes indicating the internal state, and (3) transient emotions.

The author shows how philosophical approaches to art have been made in terms of the four main systems of thought: the Nyaya, Samkhya, Vedanta, and monistic Saivist. They differ on such recurrent problems as the unity of the aesthetic object, imitation and illusion, aesthetic cognition and recognition, and the universalization of subject and object at the aesthetic level. Abhinavagupta, whom Professor Pandey seems to regard as the culmination of Indian aesthetics, since he cites few later authorities, dealt with these problems from the standpoint of the monistic Saiva philosophy of Kashmir. One of his achievements was to analyze the aesthetic personality into taste, aesthetic susceptibility, power of visualization, intellectual culture, contemplative habit, and capacity for identifying or losing oneself in the experience. Another was to show psychologically "how we rise from the empirical level to different aesthetic levels such as those of sense, imagination, emotion, catharsis, and transcendency." (p. 480f).

Some of this analysis could be, I think, expressed in terms of Western naturalistic psychology. It is a fairly common experience, for example, to find oneself increasingly engrossed and self-forgetful, in a state of "rapt attention" and vivid imagination where we cease to be sharply aware of ourselves in the theater seats and of the actors as merely imitating someone else. But in India such phenomena are given a metaphysical interpretation also and placed on a rising scale of levels up to the ideal of transcendental union with the Absolute, as in Western Neo-Platonic and Christian mysticism. In terms of medieval thought (as in Dante) art and aesthetic experience have an *anagogic* function in leading the soul upward to spiritual things. Abhinavagupta holds "that the aesthetic experience at the highest level is the experience of Self itself as pure bliss. At this level the duality of subject and object disappears through intense introversion and the basic mental state sinks back into the subconscious because it is utterly disregarded . . .The universalized 'this' shines against the universalized 'I' . . ." In passages like this, one is reminded that Abhinavagupta wrote in the 11th century and in terms which would have been congenial to Western mystics of that period.

To some extent the anagogic function of art, and the whole educational process by which a human mind can rise to a higher intellectual, moral, and aesthetic level, can be accepted as real phenomena from the naturalistic standpoint. Only in explaining that rise in terms of a spiritualistic metaphysics does the mystic part company with Western naturalism. No doubt Abhinavagupta accepted the prevailing mysticism of his time, but a great deal of what he says about aesthetic experience could be translated into Western, psychological terms with the metaphysics left out.

Many religious systems of ethics and aesthetics, Oriental and Occidental, proceed on the assumption that a higher, spiritual realm of Being exists, transcending that of empirical phenomena; also that human experience can rise to that level in some degree through the right kind of meditation, contemplation, and self-abnegation. All such systems are somewhat ascetic in depreciating the value of sensuous pleasures and attachments, including the arts. But there are many degrees of severity in such asceticism. Plato, while somewhat hostile toward "imitative" (representational) and extremely sensuous, popular art, found a place in his ideal state for the kinds of art which exerted a good moral influence and led the mind up to a grasp of universals. In Indian thought, there are countless degrees and varieties of asceticism, in general and in relation to the arts.

It is significant that Abhinavagupta was a moderate in this regard, and that Kaulism, the branch of Saivism (Siva-worship) to which he belonged, was also traditionally moderate. "It denies," says Professor Pandey,[33] "antagonism between sensuous joy and spiritual bliss (Ananda), recognizes the former to be a means to the latter, and asserts that it is meant for the few." These few have attained proficiency in Raja-Yoga as distinct from the more severely world-rejecting Hatha-Yoga. "They have such control over the mind that they can withdraw it from the stimulating object even at a time when it is being enjoyed most. A painting of Abhinavagupta, in Dr. Pandey's book about him, shows him as a musician, playing on a stringed instrument, and experiencing transcendental bliss, having attained this highest level through the imaginative, emotive, and cathartic levels. Two female attendants wait upon him with jars of Siva-Rasa, a kind of intoxicant, while dance, song, and music proceed in front of him; but his mind, says Dr. Pandey, "being in touch with the Reality, is experiencing the spiritual bliss." [34] The Krama system of Saivism "enjoins the

[33] *Abhinavagupta*, 2nd ed., p. vii.
[34] Plate IV, *Abhinavagupta Experiencing Sensuous Joy and Spiritual Bliss*, is reproduced by kind permission of Professor K. C. Pandey and his publisher from his book, *Abhinavagupta: an Historical and Philosophical Study*. Second Edition, Chowkhambra Sanskrit Series Office (Varanasi-I, India, 1963). He further explains, in a personal

use of wine, woman and meat" for ritual and philosophic purposes ("for the realization of the Real") while prohibiting it otherwise.[35] Western students of mysticism would do well to remember that Eastern mysticism is not always ascetic with regard to the sexual aspects of life and art. This is especially true of Kaulism in its Tantric aspects, which stress the female principle as source of power.[36]

Indian aesthetics seems to have stopped short in the 11th century, as to its main discoveries and original insights. Later work is more historical and critical. In his short article and in his book on *Indian Aesthetics*, Professor Pandey carries the story only to about 1200 A.D., when a philosophy of music (*Nada-Brahma-Vada*) was developed from the school of Bhartrhari (c. 650). "The philosophy of music holds that music presents the Absolute, *Nada-Brahman*, in the sensuous medium of musical sounds (*cf.* Hegel). Music is beautiful because in it the Absolute shines through the pleasant sound." (p. 485). In the philosophy of architecture, metaphysical Reality is conceived as *cosmic personality* or *cosmic order.* (p. 486). A building represents this through its own organic order, harmony, and proportion. Theories of painting follow Bharata in emphasizing the presentation of inner states and aesthetic configurations (*rasas*) through gestures, grimaces, and expressions of the eyes as in the Ajanta painting of a dancing girl. (p. 487).

Another useful work in English on the *rasa* theory is that of R. Gnoli, *The Aesthetic Experience According to*

---

letter, that the picture conforms exactly with a verbal description in verse by Madhuraja Yogin, a pupil of Abhinavagupta who was present at the scene. The verbal picture is translated into English on page 21 of *Abhinavagupta*. The painting, here reproduced in black and white, was made in 1956 in Lucknow by Mr. Sanad Chatterji under Dr. Pandey's direction and is in the latter's possession.

[35] *Abhinavagupta*, p. x.

[36] See "Shaktism," "Tantra," "Shivaism," etc., in D. Runes (ed.), *Dictionary of Philosophy* (New York, Philosophical Library, 1942).

Abhinavagupta.[37] It contains a translation of Abhinava-gupta's commentary on Bharata, which Gnoli declares to be "the most important text in the whole of Indian aesthetic thought." According to Bharata, Gnoli continues, the eight principal feelings of human nature are delight, laughter, sorrow, anger, heroism, fear, disgust, and astonishment. (Later authors added a ninth, serenity.) These nine feelings are the material of aesthetic experience, and as transformed by art become the following *rasas:* the erotic, the comic, the pathetic, the furious, the heroic, the terrible, the odious, the marvellous, and the quietistic. Things and events which cause a certain feeling in ordinary life do not arouse the corresponding one when represented on the stage or described in poetry, but color the aesthetic pleasure *(rasa)* in their own specific ways. The *rasa* theory is developed by analyzing the causes, effects, and concomitant elements of of feeling into many varieties, as occurring in ordinary life and as changed by art into different flavors or qualities. In a particular drama and the aesthetic experience it arouses, these qualities are mixed as in a dish at table, which differs from each ingredient when taken separately.[38]

"Hindu writers," says Clay Lancaster, "conceive the capacity to feel beauty (to taste *rasa*) to be the reward for merit gained in a past life. The aesthetician is born, not

[37] (Rome, Istituto per il Medio ed Estremo Oriente, 1956).

[38] *Rasa* and other concepts of Indian aesthetics are discussed in a clear and informative way by S. K. De in *Sanskrit Poetics as a Study of Aesthetic* (Berkeley, Univ. of California Press, 1963). This book deals mostly with poetry, but much of what it says is applicable to the other arts. Among the topics discussed are aesthetic enjoyment, poetic expression and imagination, creation, and re-creation. Religious aspects are not emphasized. An earlier translation of an important work on *rasa* and the drama is that of Dhanamjaya's *The Dasarupa: a Treatise on Hindu Dramaturgy*, trans. by G. C. O. Haas (New York, Columbia Univ. Press, 1912). See also M. Hiriyanna's essay, "Art Experience" in *Comparative Studies in Philosophy in Honor of Radhakrishnan* (New York, Harper, n.d.), pp. 176ff.

made. This theory is clearly enunciated in Bharata's *Vatya Sastra,* and therefore dates from at least as early as the fifth century." [39]

Ananda Coomaraswamy describes aesthetic experience as "an inscrutable and uncaused spiritual activity," brought to life as *rasa* through the spectator's own capacity. It is related to some particular work of art but not achieved through the "deliberate ordering of the work to that end." [40]

The elements of *rasa* are classified by Coomaraswamy as follows: (1) *Determinants* or physical stimulants to aesthetic reproduction; the theme and its parts; time and place; (2) *Consequents,* means of registering emotional states, as in gestures; (3) *Moods* or represented emotional states, of which thirty-three are transient (such as joy, agitation, impatience) and nine permanent. The latter are the vehicles of the specific *rasas,* one of them dominating the others; (4) Representation of *involuntary physical reactions* such as fainting.

As distinguished by Abhinavagupta and his followers, the various types of *rasa* suggest comparison with the traditional "aesthetic categories" of Western aesthetics, such as the beautiful, ugly, sublime, tragic, comic, and characteristic. These concepts have been used to describe and evaluate both works of art and the kinds of experience they arouse. In both cultures, such concepts have also functioned as aims for the artist, standards for the critic, and names for desired aesthetic responses. The types of *rasa* served to interrelate the arts, in that a particular flavor could be aroused by poetry, music, painting, sculpture, dance, or the combined art of theater.[41]

---

[39] "Keys to the Understanding of Indian and Chinese Painting," *Journal of Aesthetics and Art Criticism,* XI, 2 (Dec. 1952), p. 98n. *Cf.* Coomaraswamy, *Transformation of Nature in Art* (Cambridge, Mass., 1934), p. 55.

[40] *The Transformation of Nature in Art,* pp. 50–53.

[41] Philip Rawson's Introduction to *Music and Dance in Indian Art*

Western psychological aesthetics might profit from the attempt to distinguish and classify the types of *rasa* in a much more extensive and discriminating way. The theory as Abhinavagupta left it a thousand years ago is sure to seem highly oversimplified, rigid, and speculative to a modern psychologist. One cannot adequately reduce the varieties of aesthetic quality to any such short list of types. But the theory was based on a considerable amount of direct experience with the theater arts and their effects on an audience. The hypotheses thus derived could be further tested and developed with different kinds of audience, actors, and dramas.

The mystical element in the *rasa* theory, which makes it unacceptable as a whole to science, varies considerably from one writer to another. Coomaraswamy's account is one of the most intensely mystical and transcendental. P. J. Chaudhury's is less so. He gives two definitions, of which the first is mystical: "*Rasa* is regarded as extraordinary or unworldly; the pleasure which accompanies it as transcendental." The other is acceptable from a naturalistic point of view: "*Rasa* is realized when an emotion is awakened in the mind in such a manner that it has none of its usual conative tendencies and is experienced in an impersonal, contemplative mood." [42]

Indian music theory takes its start from the *Sama-Veda*, from which Bharata developed a system called the *Natyasastra*. (The philosophy of music, called the *Nada-Brahma-Vada*, came later.) It was developed into the classical system of *ragas* or musical modes, by way of the octave with its tones and semitones, consonant and dissonant intervals,

---

(Edinburgh, Royal Scottish Museum, 1963), discusses the theory of *rasa* in relation to several arts.

[42] "The Theory of *Rasa*," *Journal of Aesthetics and Art Criticism*, XI, 2 (Dec. 1952), p. 147; also "Catharsis in the Light of Indian Aesthetics," *JAAC*, XV, 2 (Dec. 1956), p. 215.

gramas or basic scales, and *jatis* or basic modes.[43] Pitch is relative. A *raga* is a mode which has developed a certain distinctive ethos or emotional mood such as sadness or exuberance, usually as a result of certain pivotal notes which are selected as the beginning, middle, and end of the melody.[44]

In late North Indian music, the *ragas* came to suggest particular divine or human beings, male and female (*raga*, *ragini*), times of day or night, seasons, and appropriate moods. These were portrayed in paintings such as the Rajput miniatures, thus providing another way of interrelating the arts.[45] Thirty-six or more *ragas* and *raginis* were distinguished, necessitating elaborate classifications.

Sources of Indian Tradition contains an informative section on "Aesthetic Speculations" under the heading of "Kama, the Third End of Man." This, explains V. Raghavan, is "the pursuit of love and pleasure in the balanced scheme of life," especially in the stage of life attained by the married householder.[46] Pleasure is to be controlled as part of a well-balanced life experience. Human love symbolizes

[43] A. Bake, "The Music of India," in E. Wellesz (ed.), *Ancient and Oriental Music* (London, 1957), pp. 195ff. Also C. Sachs, *The Rise of Music in the Ancient World* (New York, 1943), pp. 105ff; A. H. Fox Strangways, *The Music of Hindostan* (Oxford, 1914); S. Bandopadyaya, *The Music of India* (Bombay, Taraporevala, n.d.); W. G. Raffé, "Ragas and Raginis: a Key to Indian Aesthetics," *Journal of Aesthetics and Art Criticism*, XI, 2 (Dec. 1952), pp. 105–117.

[44] A. Bake, *loc. cit.*, pp. 204, 213. On *rasas* and *ragas* in Indian music and painting, see A. Bake, "Aesthetics of Indian Music," *British Journal of Aesthetics*, IV, 1 (Jan. 1964), pp. 47–57.

[45] On the relation between musical and pictorial *ragas*, see O. C. Gangoly's well-illustrated book, *Ragas and Raginis* (Bombay, Nalanda Pubs., 1948). Also H. J. Stooke and K. Khandavala, *The Laud Ragamala Miniatures* (Oxford, B. Cassirer, 1953); M. S. Randhawa, *Kangra Paintings on Love* (New Delhi, National Museum, 1962).

[46] The other three main ends, according to Hinduism, are *Dharma* or the organization of social and individual life, *Artha* or material gain and polity, and *Moksha* or release of the soul from matter and rebirth. (*Sources of Indian Tradition*, chs. IX, X, XI).

the seeking by the individual of the Supreme Soul, and this is symbolized in erotic visual art. By thus reconciling and merging the pleasures of physical love with religious aspiration, Hinduism avoided much of the anxiety over sin, the conflict between sensual and spiritual, which have troubled the Hebrew and Christian conscience for millennia. The more enlightened minds would be conscious of the spiritual meaning, even in the midst of sensual enjoyment; others would experience the latter in a more corporeal way.

"Hindu aesthetics," Mr. Raghavan adds, "explained the philosophy of beauty in terms of the enjoyment or perception of a state of sublime composure or blissful serenity which was a reflection, intimation, image, or glimpse of the enduring bliss of the spirit . . ." Vatsyayana's *Kama Sutra* describes the "man of taste and culture" who enjoys the good things of this world with developed aesthetic taste as a member of cultivated society. But speculations on beauty and art go back to the Vedas, Brahmanas, and Upanishads, as well as to the epics, *Ramayana* and *Mahabharata*. The highest type of drama was conceived as the heroic play of gods and heroes, incarnations of the Supreme Deity; it had a moral, didactic role, but this was subordinated to that of aesthetic enjoyment. The varieties of such enjoyment and their causes in art and human nature were set forth by the theoreticians.[47]

Painting in India, says Clay Lancaster,[48] goes back to

[47] *Sources of Indian Tradition* contains excerpts from the works of Bharata (*Treatise on Dramaturgy*), Mammata (*Illuminations of Poetry*), c. 1100 A.D., Jagannatha (*The Ocean of Aesthetic Emotion*), from the ancient poets, and from musical treatises. On *Kama* and the *Kama-Sutra* in relation to Indian painting and sculpture, see M. R. Anand, *Kama Kala* (New York, Nagel, 1958); P. Thomas, *Kama Kalpa* (Bombay, Taraporevala, n.d.); and M. S. Randhawa, *Kangra Paintings on Love* (New Delhi, 1962).

[48] "Keys to the Understanding of Indian and Chinese Painting: the 'Six Limbs' of Yasodhara and the 'Six Principles' of Hsieh Ho,"

ancient times, being mentioned in the *Ramayana*. The oldest historical account of it says there was a decline in the third century A.D. After the Gupta period, ideas on the subject began to be systematized. A twelfth-century writer named Yasodhara recorded a Sanskrit couplet describing the six "limbs" or component parts of painting. It is inserted in Book I, Chapter II of a commentary on the second-century *Kama Sutra* of Vatsayana, and may be dated in the sixth or seventh century.

This couplet is translated as follows: "Differentiation of types, canons of proportion, embodiment of sentiment and charm, correspondence of formal and pictorial elements, preparation (lit. 'breaking,' 'analysis') of pigments; these are the six limbs of painting." [49] The first point, says Mr. Lancaster, refers to subject, the second to composition, the third to the artist's response during the process of painting, the fourth to that which is grasped by the spectator, the fifth to content, and the sixth to the mechanics of production. "Breaking" in the sixth refers not only to the preparation of pigments, but to the "three breakings" or bends of the body in the classical dance pose. These Indian concepts closely resemble the Chinese "Six Principles," to be described in a later section of this book.

Types of painting are distinguished in the Indian texts as suitable for temples, palaces, or private dwellings; also as "true, lyrical, and secular." Right proportions are

Journal of Aesthetics and Art Criticism, XI, 2 (Dec. 1952), pp. 95–104. This article summarizes and compares the traditional Indian and Chinese principles of painting and provides a copious bibliography on both subjects. The amount of Hindu writing on painting is itself "staggering." Only a small fraction has been translated.

[49] Coomaraswamy, *Transformation of Nature in Art*, pp. 181–182. Another set of "limbs," eight in number, is more technical: the brush, preparation of the ground, outline work, characteristic lineaments of the types, production or coloring, shading and plastic modeling, corrections, and final outlines.

stressed, as in the Ajanta cave paintings (c. seventh century A.D.).[50] Three kinds of shading are described in the *Vishnudharmottaram;* they vary from faint washes and stipples to the suggestion of high relief. This text emphasized the importance for painting of a knowledge of the dance.

The Ajanta paintings, as Benjamin Rowland points out, came at a time when Buddhism had gone from the early (Hinayana) stage to the theistic Mahayana stage, in which Buddha had assumed the stature of an eternal god. In early Buddhism it had been believed "that he who had gone beyond the fetters of the body could not be endowed by art with the likeness of a body"; but later a deified Buddha image was developed along with the cult of the Bodhisattvas. These figure prominently in the Ajanta paintings. *Sastras* or manuals of artistic practice specified the relative sizes and proportions of the figures and the ways in which parts of the body were to be shown. (E.g., Buddha's eyes are to be like lotus petals, his arching brows like the curve of the bow.) The material culture of India at the Gupta and Chaluka periods is well represented, says Professor Rowland; for example, with rich textiles, jewelry, and palace architecture. The Indian principle of *bhava,* or dramatic expression of emotions through poses and gestures, and also that of continuous narration, are illustrated in the picture of Raja and his fainting Queen (Cave XVII). Paintings of the Ajanta type are thought to have had a strong influence on Buddhist art in China and Turkestan.

Of special interest for the comparison of Indian and Western aesthetics are two recent articles in English: the first by Philip Rawson on "The Methods of Indian Sculpture.[50a]

---

[50] See the Introduction by Benjamin Rowland to *The Ajanta Caves: Early Buddhist Paintings from India* (New York, Mentor-Unesco, 1963), esp. pp. 7ff.

[50a] *Asian Review,* New Series, I, 3 (Dec. 1964), pp. 115–127.

Mr. Rawson notes that the concept of rasa was combined by later commentators with *harsha*, the condition of joy which arises in the spectator in response to rasa. He credits Anandavardhana with the concept of *dhvani*, the overtones or mental resonance which sounds or forms evoke, over and above their prose sense. An enlightening analysis of Indian sculpture by Mr. Rawson emphasizes the intellectual aspects of its formal invention. They include *plastic* or static spatial forms and *linear* or sequential temporal forms. All the units of form into which the surfaces of Indian sculpture are divided are convex; the form expresses a reality dependent on its containing space, and invites the spectator to self-identification. Indian sculpture is fundamentally in relief. Its contours are developed as the loci of continuously moving lines, which gives an effect of suavity and fluidity. Coherence is sought within individual figures; also between them and the visual field. Tactile suggestions, strong lighting, and ideal proportions of the human figure are important.

R. Morton Smith adds, in the same issue (pp. 150–159), some challenging "contrasts between Sanskrit and Western literatures." His emphasis is on the Indian idea that words contain the secret of creative power. The range of poetic subjects is limited in India. The status of poetry since the classics is low, says Mr. Smith; no new moral or religious light is expected from it, and its aim is pleasure. "Language, as part of sensual beauty, partakes of unreality and leads to further karma." Since the Veda tradition can tell everything, there is no call for wonder, discovery, or new thought. Much secular Sanskrit literature before Kalidasa (400 A.D.) may have been lost. Freedom of thought was circumscribed "by the brain-washing of orthodoxy." Individual personality is disliked and distrusted; not prized for originality. The individual is unreal and valueless. The idea of poetry as

42

self-expression is impossible in India, since knowing Brahma is a guarantee of release. There is no faith in man or nature as good. Creation is in technique and verbal ornament, not spiritual depth, and this is dehumanizing. The various spheres of culture cannot cross-fertilize one another, and the culture has become ossified. There is little interest in character and its development; types are static and unchanging, Mr. Smith declares.

The approach to art and beauty by way of *Kama*, as concerned with the earthly, empirical, sensuous level of experience, brings Indian aesthetics closer to certain Western attitudes and interests than the more metaphysical approaches do. The *Kama Sutra* provides much worldly wisdom and technique on amatory matters, which parallel Western treatises in ancient Rome and the Renaissance. These subjects have been treated with increasing frankness in Western art, especially literature, but have never played a major part in the more ascetic, intellectual traditions which have dominated Western aesthetics as a branch of philosophy. The extant writings of Plato, Aristotle, and even Epicurus are all somewhat austere on erotic matters.

This is but one indication of the persistent gulf between Western art and Western aesthetics. It finds theoretical expression in the usual restriction of art and aesthetic experience to the "higher senses." "Aesthetic experience" is commonly defined so as to exclude ordinary, physical desires and satisfactions. Bharata held, says Dr. Pandey, "that eye and ear are the only aesthetic senses . . . On this point some of the Western aestheticians, such as St. Thomas, Addison, and Kant agree." [51] To Vatsyayana and other, less ascetic theorists in both East and West, *ars amatoria* is an art and can be developed as such. The "lower" senses of touch, taste, and smell are capable of aesthetic experience in a broad sense

[51] "Indian Aesthetics," p. 474.

of the term. On the whole, Indian aesthetics has agreed with Indian art in approving realistic eroticism in art, on condition that it is disciplined, refined, and ordered. Insistence on its religious and cosmic symbolism helps to do this, but introduces no strong tendency to inner conflict, shame, or sense of sin. The innate limitations of the lower senses in perceiving complex form are recognized by psychologists everywhere, but that has not prevented Eastern art from endowing lower sense-qualities, such as those of perfume, with meanings which tend to dignify, refine, and incorporate them in the realm of fine art.

Although Indian aesthetics does not seem to have changed or developed fundamentally since the thirteenth century, some important and original treatises on contemporary art from a philosophical point of view are still being written there. I have in mind especially *The Social Function of Art* by Radhakamal Mukerjee of Lucknow University.[52] This author has published a long list of books, mostly on the economics and sociology of modern India, but including several which touch upon the arts. These are, for example, *The Theory and Art of Mysticism* and *The Social Structure of Values*. Dr. Mukerjee's approach is theoretical, not historical, while drawing at the same time upon a rich knowledge of cultural history. He manifests an impressive knowledge of the arts of East and West in all periods. He is well read in Western psychology and psychoanalysis, social science and aesthetics, as well as Oriental philosophy. He applies this knowledge to world art in many media. Professor Mukerjee is essentially Indian in his outlook and assumptions, but he treats Occidental civilization with unusual understanding.

[52] Bombay, Hind Kitabs Ltd., 1948.

44

8. Traditional Japanese aesthetic concepts

It is interesting to find in Japanese writings on art persistent references to certain other aesthetic qualities which invite comparison with the Indian *rasas*. One of these is called *aware*, which has been translated as "nostalgic emotionalism," "gentle melancholy" or "sensitivity to the beautiful sadness of things." It refers especially to that quality as it is found in outside objects, not as a purely inward feeling. Western psychologists would say that the feeling is projected upon, or attributed to, the outside object as one of its aesthetic qualities. This implies a certain harmony between the human heart and mind on one hand, and on the other the outside world of appearances and forms, often brief but capable of arousing sudden joy or grief. Motoori Norinaga, in the late eighteenth century, regarded this quality as essential in literature of the Heian period and especially in the *Genji Monogatari*.[53] That novel as a whole, he said, was pervaded by *mono no aware* as a "sensitivity to things," such as the fall of a flower or an unwept tear.

Some other concepts of aesthetic qualities, attributed to aristocratic literature of the Heian and later periods, are *en* (charming), *okashi* (cheerful, amusing), and *miyabi* (pleasant in a quiet, refined, tasteful way). Their meanings

[53] An example is the passage in Waley's translation of *Genji*, I, Ch. IV, pp. 100–101. There is a discussion with references to Japanese writing in Frits Vos, *A Study of the Ise-Monogatari*, I, Introduction (The Hague, Mouton, 1957), pp. 8–9. Vos quotes Tsugita Uru as saying that the ideal of *mono no aware* became the ideal of literature and the principle of life of the aristocracy. Norinaga states that it developed into a kind of ideology, with more and more restricted meanings. In the words of Hisamatsu Sen'ichi, *mono no aware* is "the spirit of nostalgic emotionalism discovered in things"; it is the world of sentiments discovered in the harmony between heart (mind) and objects. *Aware* is not restricted to sadness: it includes bright feelings on a spring morning, as well as sadness on an autumn evening.

changed slightly, but were roughly in contrast with *makoto* (plain sincerity).[54] An old term which took on a special aesthetic meaning late in the medieval period was *sabi*. It was associated with the peculiar beauty of old, faded, worn, or lonely things.[55]

Another influential concept in Japanese theories of art is *yügen*. It summarized the aesthetic ideals of the Kamakura period, and was used "to describe the profound, remote, and mysterious, those things which can not easily be grasped or expressed in words." [56] It suggests a vague, indefinite symbolism. This conception developed actively, as did that of *rasa*, in the serious drama. It was theoretically explained by the great playwright, actor, and manager Seami (1363–1443), who was responsible for many of the Noh plays. He made of the Noh a "symbolic theater, in which the most important actions were not represented but suggested." The main character is often a ghost or spirit from another world. Dance and gesture may suggest the distance of the world of the dead and the anguish of being born.

Yügen in the sense of mysterious power had been used as a standard of criticism, but Seami developed it into a "unifying aesthetic principle, underlying all parts of the Noh." [57] It implied a certain kind of spiritual power, achieved only in the highest realms of art. It was conceived in accordance with the principles of Zen, and applied to both the external object, the work of art, and the feelings it aroused.

Makoto Ueda explains some further implications of *yügen* in Seami's thought.[58] It is "the inner beauty of an object

[54] *Sources of the Japanese Tradition,* Chs. IX, XIV, XIX.
[55] P. 286.
[56] *Sources,* p. 284.
[57] P. 289.
[58] M. Ueda, "Zeami on Art: a Chapter for the History of Japanese

outwardly expressed by means of art . . . the manifestation of the 'primary meaning' which lies in the mysterious depth of things . . . the truth caught by the artist's soul." It combines the ideas of elegant beauty and sad resignation, the latter from recognizing man's helplessness before cosmic power and mutability. This sense of *yügen* is also called "sublimity," as in the calm, subdued beauty of old age. Art tries to illuminate the depths of the human mind, beyond the reach of the senses. Seami assumes, says Mr. Ueda, the animistic conception of a collective mind throughout the cosmos. His aesthetics combines elements of Shintoism, Confucianism, Buddhism, Chinese and Japanese poetics and calligraphy.

As in India, China, and the West, the drama and poetry were at first regarded by Japanese aestheticians as having a didactic, moral, and social purpose. But in all parts of the world, long experience with didactic art showed that high moral aims were not enough; aesthetic power was also necessary.

Writing of the seventeenth-century poet Bashō, Makoto Ueda brings out some aesthetic ideas expressed in the Haiku. (This is one of the shortest of all verse-forms, consisting of three lines with seventeen syllables). Bashō, who originated it, emphasized a "transpersonal" ideal of poetry, in which the poet's ego is dissolved by submerging itself within a natural object. He perceives its life, feels its feelings, and out of this the poem emerges; object and poet must not be two separate things. The energy of the universe is transpersonal in having no personal emotion; the poet suppresses purely human elements in himself. Other aesthetic ideas advanced by Bashō, says Professor Ueda, are

Aesthetics," *Journal of Aesthetics and Art Criticism*, XX, 1 (Fall 1961), pp. 73–79.

sabi, shiori, hosomi; inspiration, fragrance, reverberation, reflection, and lightness. *Sabi* is derived from *sabishi,* meaning "lonely" or "desolate." [59]

Typical principles of Eastern (especially Japanese) and Western architecture are contrasted by Clay Lancaster with reference to their religious and philosophic associations.[60] One is the solidarity of Western construction as compared with the apparent fragility of Eastern. This is in line with Lao Tzu's teaching "that to be alive is to be pliant, that stiffness is death, and to preserve tenderness in lieu of becoming hardened by life is a sign of having great strength." Professor Lancaster mentions eight significant differences between Western and Eastern: "(1) that the first has the appearance of solidarity and the second that of lightness; (2) that the one considers the building from the point of view of form and the other from that of volume; (3) that the first is composed of individualized parts and the second of integrated units; (4) that the former shows a tendency to embellish and the latter an inclination to simplify; (5) that Western building designs stress verticality and the Eastern horizontality; (6) that Occidental architects stand on a formal footing with their work and the Oriental architects establish a close association with it; (7) that the first is more concerned with effects and the second a forthright exhibit of materials, and (8) that in the West a building is withdrawn from the natural environment whereas in the Far East it is identified with the setting." All of these are linked with far-reaching cultural attitudes.

[59] M. Ueda, "Bashō and the Poetics of 'Haiku,'" *Journal of Aesthetics and Art Criticism,* XXI, 4 (Summer 1963), pp. 423–431.

[60] "Metaphysical Beliefs and Architectural Principles," *Journal of Aesthetics and Art Criticism,* XIV, 2 (Mar. 1956), pp. 287–303. G. B. Mohan discusses this article and compares Indian and Japanese theories of poetry in a letter to the Editor, *JAAC,* XXII, 3 (Spring 1964), p. 336.

It is not yet evident to what extent Eastern architects or aestheticians have become conscious and purposeful along such lines, or motivated by religio-philosophic world-views. People seldom become fully conscious of their own cultural traits and the significance of their artistic styles until they have encountered very different ones in some other cultural group or period. Even when the aesthetic principles behind an art have not been explicitly written out by critics and philosophers, they may be gradually brought up to the conscious level by comparative analyses. This requires a sympathetic understanding of the cultural backgrounds as well as of the arts themselves.

Japanese art of the Ukiyo-e style in the seventeenth and later centuries was in a somewhat popular, naturalistic, decorative spirit, portraying the worldly, sensuous pleasures of the "floating world." But this also had a moral and religious symbolism for the Buddhist, in illustrating the ephemeral nature of worldly pleasures. The interest of the floating world in sex and money was partly counterbalanced by the ideal of *giri* or moral obligation for self-control, as dramatized in the plays of Chikamatsu.[61]

D. T. Suzuki, contemporary interpreter of Zen, gives a religious meaning to some of these aesthetic concepts.[62] He links them to *kannagara*, the acceptance of things as they come; the Way which is natural to the gods; a spiritual yielding to Amida Buddha through "absolute passivity." *Sabi*, according to Dr. Suzuki, is a feeling of absolute aloneness in one's own individual self. *Aware* is an emotional, sentimental response to nature. Various emotions move in us as the seasons alternate.

[61] *Sources*, pp. 443ff.
[62] "Japanese Thought," in *History of Philosophy East and West*, Ch. XXV.

Zen and the Fine Arts, by Shin'ichi Hisamatsu,[63] is said by a reviewer to be "the only substantial work devoted entirely to Zen and its integral relationship to the fine arts." The author contends that seven unique characteristics of Zen are to be found in cultural products influenced by that philosophy. They exist "simultaneously and interpenetratively." These are: (1) *fukinsei* (asymmetry), (2) *kanso* (simplicity), (3) *kokō* (austerity and storied witheredness), (4) *shizen* (naturalness), (5) *yūgen* (profundity), (6) *datsuzoku* (detachment or non-formalism), and (7) *seijaku* (tranquillity). The structure of the Grand Shinto Shrine at Ise, says the author, lacks such Zen characteristics as asymmetry, detachment, austerity, and storied witheredness.

Each of the traditional names for aesthetic qualities took on slightly different nuances of mood and feeling as used by different writers and periods, and as applied to different objects of nature and art. The same can be said of *rasa* in India and of "beauty" and "sublimity" in Europe.

9. Some traditional Chinese theories of painting

The Japanese concept of *yūgen* as a mysterious, psychic power in art has something in common with the Chinese ideal of "spirit resonance" in painting. This ideal was first among the famous "Six Principles" laid down by Hsieh Ho at the end of the fifth century A.D. Its precise implications have long been debated by sinologists. Osvald Sirèn defines

[63] (Kyoto, Bokubisha, 1958). The author is an active Zenist and has taught Zen and other Asiatic philosophies at the University of Kyoto. It contains 290 plates and 106 pages of text, mostly in Japanese. It discusses aspects of Zen as related to painting, calligraphy, architecture, floral arrangement, gardens, craftwork, and the drama. See the review by Kenneth K. Inada in *Philosophy East and West*, Jan. 1963, p. 361.

it as a "vibration or consonance of the vitalizing spirit and movement of life," and again as "a cosmic, spiritual force imparting life, character, and significance to material forms, linking the individual artist with cosmic force." It refers primarily to psychic forces within the artist and communicated by him to the work of art. It is an "echo from his divine, creative genius reverberating in the lines and shapes which he draws with his hand." [64]

Every connoisseur of painting will agree that there is a subtle but crucial difference between brushstrokes which seem "alive," communicating vitality, and those which seem dead or flaccid. The same can be said of different passages in poetry and music, and of the performer's rendition of them. The concept has thus been applied to various arts. It is somewhat subjective, since "vitality" and "vibration" are qualities the observer can project upon the work of art from his own empathetic responses. Experts do not agree entirely on which works possess the most spirit resonance, and they did not agree in ancient China. But the concept is also partly objective, in that some examples tend more strongly to stimulate that type of response in a trained observer; others an opposite one. The artist himself was expected to perceive and portray the "spiritual qualities" in each concrete object, such as a gnarled old pine-tree, which give it a distinctive kind of life and character.[65]

[64] *The Chinese on the Art of Painting* (Peiping, Vetch, 1936), pp. 19, 23. On Hsieh Ho, Kuo Hsi and other early Chinese writers on painting, see also S. Sakanishi (trans.), *An Essay on Landscape Painting* and *The Spirit of the Brush* (London, Murray, Wisdom of the East Series, 1935, 1939).

[65] Wing-tsit Chan recounts a Taoist anecdote about a painter with casual manners at court. From it is derived the phrase "taking off clothes and squatting down bare-backed." This, says Professor Chan, expresses "a basic principle of Chinese art." It means "that art is dedicated to the expression of the inner spirit instead of physical verisimilitude and that painting should be a spontaneous and instantaneous flow of the brush." *Source Book of Chinese Philosophy* (Princeton, 1963), p. 210.

The other five principles stated by Hsieh Ho are (2) bone manner or structural use of the brush; (3) conformity with objects to give likeness; (4) application of colors according to the characteristics; (5) plan and design, place and position (composition); (6) transmission of models by drawing. Of the Six Principles, Sirèn remarks that, although not new with Hsieh Ho, "they contain the essentials of the traditional attitude, and they were never entirely discarded or replaced by any other principles of corresponding importance." [66] In addition, many writers on painting from pre-T'ang times to the present have emphasized the classical, Confucian ideal of art as conducive to right conduct. One of these, Chang Yen-yüan (c. 845 A.D.) gave a more specific, metaphysical interpretation to the Six Principles, especially the first. It was "a spiritual force imparting life, character and significance to material forms, something that links the works of the individual artist with a cosmic principle." It is "active in the artist before it becomes manifest in his works . . . like an echo from the divine part of his creative genius reverberating in the lines and shapes which he draws from his hand." [67] Confucian, Taoist, and Buddhist philosophers agreed that "to understand the meaning of a thing, one must become the thing, harmonize one's consciousness with it and reach the mental attitude which brings knowledge without intellectual deliberation." Then the subjective and objective are identical.

The first principle, Sirèn explains, is the most inclusive formula for the essentials of painting. It contains the ideas of life-breath, cosmic vitality, harmonious vibrations, birth, and movements of life. On the second principle (structural brushwork), Sirèn comments that it has always been accepted as an element of primary importance in Chinese painting—the *sine qua non* of the painter's technical ac-

[66] P. 19.
[67] P. 23.

complishments." (Brushstroke is more important in Chinese than in Western painting.) The third (conform with objects in order to give likeness) demands more objective correspondence with nature, but not exact realism; rather, a spirit or symbolic meaning to be expressed through the form of a certain kind of object.

Professor Clay Lancaster, whom I have quoted above on the "Six Limbs" of Indian painting, summarizes the six Chinese principles as follows: "first, spirit; second, structure-technique; third, representation; fourth, appearance; fifth, composition; and sixth, method of learning." [68] He goes on to rearrange the twelve concepts in pairs, each dealing with the same general idea. "The idea in the Chinese principle of spirit (1) relates to the Indian of expression (3), the Chinese technique (2) to the Indian use of materials (6), the Chinese concern with subject (3) to the Indian insistence upon recognizing objects (5), and Hsieh Ho's composition (5) to Yasodhara's proportion and placing—'measurement' (2)." There are also differences. "The Chinese begins with spirit, the Indian with form-distinction, which has no approximate correspondence in Chinese laws . . . The other omission is the fourth Indian component, the infusion of grace and charm." The Indian recognizes no importance in copying works of art, and does not emphasize technical dexterity. The Indian conceives form primarily in terms of proportion, the Chinese in terms of placing.

A fairly long, detailed Chinese work on the history of painting is Kuo Jo-Hsü's *Experiences in Painting*, translated with notes by A. C. Soper.[69] Written in the eleventh century, it is full of theoretical generalities—among them

[68] *Op. cit.*, pp. 103–104.
[69] (Washington, D. C., American Council of Learned Societies, 1951). See also A. C. Soper, "The First Two Laws of Hsieh Ho," *The Far Eastern Quarterly*, VIII, 4 (Aug. 1949), p. 423.

the statement (p. 15) that "spirit consonance" cannot be taught, being innate. The author takes a moderate stand on the question of progress or decline in art: "Modern times have fallen behind in some respects, but also have made further progress in others." (p. 21). Kuo lists a considerable number of painters, classifying them as to provenance, and characterizes them briefly, praising some and disparaging others. His evaluations are disappointingly vague as to standards of value.

Tracing old pictures was common, and the fact that capable artists did so often makes it hard to distinguish originals from copies today. In copying, some originality was not always discouraged. Sakanishi (p. 25) quotes Ku K'ai-chih as saying "If the brush and eye travel boldly forward, the copy will not be a mere reproduction, but will contain something of the copyist's own." Nevertheless, there was little call for radical innovation, as compared with that in modern Western culture. Here individual originality is often taken as the highest aim of the artist and the chief standard of value in judging his art; also as a major aim in art education.

Wen Fong has critically reviewed the long controversy over the Six Principles in a concise article, "On Hsieh Ho's 'Liu-fa.' " [70] They are not, he concludes, a coherent critical schema. "Of the six, only the first 'Fa' [method] can be said to deal squarely with qualities." The second, third, and fifth, says Dr. Fong, name the principal parts of Chinese painting without evaluative implications: i.e., brushwork, representation, coloring, and composition. The sixth is on copying as an important, separate art. A good copy must

---

[70] *Oriental Art*, IX, 4 (Winter 1963), pp. 242–245. *Cf.* W. R. B. Acker, *Some T'ang and Pre-T'ang Texts on Chinese Painting* (Leiden, 1954), pp. xxiii, 4.

PLATE V. *A Harpist*. Chinese, T'ang Dynasty, terracotta.
(The Cleveland Museum of Art, Edward L. Whittemore Fund).

show excellence in these parts of painting; to be superlative it must "also convey that elusive, immortal quality of 'spirit-resonance—'life-motion.' "

The Six Principles are somewhat analogous, Dr. Fong continues, to a Western list of "rules" and "parts" of painting devised by Anton Mengs in the 18th century. Instead of "spirit-resonance," Mengs gives "harmony and grace"; instead of "brushwork" he gives "chiaroscuro," and instead of "copy-making," "proportions of the human body."

In an essay called "Preface on Landscape Painting," Tsung Ping (375–443 A.D.) expressed an ideal which dominated early Chinese work in that art. This, says James Cahill,[71] was "to arouse in the viewer those emotions that the actual scene would arouse." Viewing a landscape was an imaginary journey. The forms of nature have immaterial qualities of attractiveness or "flavor," said Tsung Ping. (Compare the Indian concept of *rasa*.) These affect the sensitive observer. By the eleventh century the main interest of painters had shifted from man to nature, where it remained. But, Mr. Cahill continues, in the late eleventh century the ideal shifted to using the arts as vehicles for embodying one's personal thought and feeling; for conveying to others something of one's own nature.[72] Poetry, music, and calligraphy had long been treated so, and now Su Shih (1036–1101) led a group of scholar-artists who applied the principle to painting. Many new, "untrammeled" styles expressed the personal qualities of different artist, rather than the nature or appearance of the objects represented. (This anticipates Western romanticism, as some early T'ang art had anticipated modern "action painting.") However, Chinese painting never lost touch with nature

[71] *Chinese Painting* (Skira, Switzerland, 1960), pp. 25, 29.
[72] *Ibid.*, p. 89.

to the extent of becoming purely abstract or non-objective. Calligraphy was non-representational, but retained its linguistic meanings.

Professor Soper has dealt with the question of standards, a central one in any system of aesthetics, in a separate article.[73] Here he analyzes several other traditional works, notably the *Critique of Famous Painters of the Sung Dynasty* by Liu Tao-ch'un. Northern Sung painting, he remarks, was dominated by the Imperial Academy, comparable to that of Louis XIV. In figure painting, it perpetuated a three-century-old style with definite rules which, Mr. Soper comments, would not have disturbed Sir Joshua Reynolds. High ratings went to artists who obeyed the classical rules with only slight deviation. Disapproval went to those who practiced bizarre styles or chose too-popular subjects. The qualities sought were "form, movement, and the sense of inner life." Color was deemed unnecessary and vulgar in figure painting, says Mr. Soper.

In landscape painting, individualism was rife. Standards were vague and poetic or mystical. Here, too, color was unnecessary in achieving the principal goals of solidarity, spaciousness, and permanence.[74] The late rise of flower

[73] "Standards of Quality in Northern Sung Painting," *Archives of the Chinese Art Society of America*, XI (1957), p. 8.

[74] Mrs. Margaret Marcus of The Cleveland Museum of Art holds a different conception of the role of color in Chinese painting. "Color appears consistently in Chinese painting," she writes, "in both religious and secular works." Mrs. Marcus quotes Hsieh Ho as saying, "according to species apply color." Examples of colorful Sung painting, she adds, are to be found in Hui Ts'ung's *Women Preparing Silk* (Boston Museum of Fine Arts) and *Barbarians Adoring Shakyamuni* (Cleveland Museum of Art; Northern Sung Dynasty, attributed to Chao Kuang-fu). A detail from a hanging scroll in the Cleveland Museum is reproduced in color on the cover of the *Bulletin* of that Museum for January, 1962. It is from *Lady Hsüan-wên-chün Giving Instructions on the Classics*, by Ch'en Hung-shou (1598–1652). See the accompanying article by Wai-kam Ho, "Nan-Ch'en Pei-Tsui," with

painting, under high patronage, produced a "split between two ideals." One, says Mr. Soper, revived the early love of Chinese art for sensuous coloring, as in porcelains and silks, which had long been inhibited by the austere scholars' preference for black-and-white ink drawing. Some scholars continued to find in the black-and-white medium a sufficient outlet for the Taoist ideal of freedom, in striving for "sketchy spontaneity." Others (notably Chao Ch'ang) broke away entirely from the figure-painting tradition to achieve "miraculous effects of color and life." This inconsistency, says Mr. Soper, was never fully reconciled in theory.[75]

It must be agreed that China placed an unusually strong emphasis on landscape painting in black ink with little or no color, from the Sung dynasty on. Japan did likewise in the Muromachi period under Chinese influence.[76] From a theoretical standpoint, the main question is, perhaps, not the extent to which color was avoided, but the reasons for doing so. Comparable trends in Western art can be found in Greek vase painting and in sculpture from the Hellenistic period to the present. At certain times and places the taste for polychromy prevails within a given art; at others not. When rejected in one art, it is often cultivated in others at the same time. When it is rejected, an emphasis on expressive form in two or three dimensions may prevail instead. Different reasons are given at the time, none of them wholly adequate.

---

details about the styles and theoretical ideals of some late Ming painters. Mr. Ho emphasizes the clash between individualistic intuition and obedience to the old masters.

[75] Another recent work in English on the theory of Chinese painting is by Mai-mai Sze, *The Tao of Painting* (New York, Pantheon, 1956). It contains a translation of *The Mustard Seed Garden Manual of Painting* (1679–1701), in a later edition; also an explanation of traditional ideals, motives, symbols, and techniques. It is handsomely printed and illustrated, but the translation has been criticized.

[76] See Sherman E. Lee, *Japanese Decorative Style*, p. 48.

The recent French contribution to our knowledge of Oriental aesthetics (which I have not tried to cover in detail) is represented by Nicole Vandier-Nicolas in *Art et sagesse en Chine: Mi Fou (1051–1107)*.[77] The subject of her book (in English, Mi Fu or Mi Fei) was a painter and connoisseur of art in the Northern Sung period, one of the independent scholar-painters who played an influential role in the art and aesthetics of that troubled age. He wrote on both painting and literature. Madame Vandier-Nicolas, who is learned in Chinese and Sanskrit, places her subject in a long perspective of Indian and Chinese aesthetics through the Manchu period.

Mme. Vandier-Nicolas writes as a mystic in the traditions of Indian aesthetics and of Ch'an and Zen. She attributes a mystic-religious attitude to Mi Fu—much more than Osvald Sirèn does, for example.[78] Painting for the scholar-painters involved, she thinks, "direct contact with the ineffable and revelation, through the veil of art, of a reality beyond speech." (p. 3). "Mystic intuition alone can open the road . . . leading to communion with the principle of life in the bosom of the All." "Art leads to knowledge of the fundamental self where the world is reflected; toward discovery of the absolute source." (p. 6).

I leave it to experts in the field to decide how mystical Mi Fu and his contemporaries really were. However, I believe that a Western connoisseur does not need to be a mystic in order to understand and appreciate their paintings and their theories.

James F. Cahill, of the Freer Gallery in Washington, takes issue with the common view that Confucianism in painting produced a dry academicism, while the more spontaneous, untrammeled styles were fostered by Taoism

[77] (Paris, Presses Universitaires, 1963).
[78] *The Chinese on the Art of Painting*, index refs. on Mi Fei (Fu).

and Ch'an Buddhism.[79] The earliest extant references to painting, he says, from the Han and Six Dynasties periods, give it an illustrative, a magical, and a moral function. The early Confucianist emphasis on traditional, moral subject-matter was short-lived. Neo-Taoism led to the view of paintings as abstractions of visual impressions into images and also as embodying the artist's feelings toward his subject; the emotional responses it calls forth.

Later Confucianists developed the idea of art as revealing the nature of the individual artist, and as expressing what is too subtle or strong for direct verbal statement. Calligraphy, like painting, expresses and communicates what is ineffable in words. The lines, colors, and textures of painting can serve as expressive means independently of the subject-matter. This differs from the early Confucian emphasis on moral subjects in art. Painting became an integral part of the humanist tradition. The superior man could respond to outer objects and project his feelings into them temporarily, without abiding concern or excessive attachment to the objects themselves.

10. Chinese theories of literature

Two famous and highly influential works in this field have recently been put into English. One is Lu Chi's "Wen Fu," written about 302 A.D.; the other is a more comprehensive work by Liu Hsieh, over a century later, which has been translated as *The Literary Mind and the Carving of Dragons.*[80]

---

[79] "Confucian Elements in the Theory of Painting," in *The Confucian Persuasion*, ed. by A. F. Wright (Stanford, Calif., Stanford Univ. Press, 1960), pp. 115–140.

[80] As usual, there is some dispute over the correct translation of both these classics. A widely known rendering of the "Wen Fu" is

Lu Chi is in the Confucian tradition as to veneration of the past, but at the same time an individualist with the will and ability to be original. He warns against two faults —excessive ornamentation and dryness or weakness through lack of feeling. There must be order and proportion between the subject, the emotions expressed, the wording, and the form.

The *Wen Fu* is a short, concise prose poem on "the superb artistries achieved by the writers before us" and "the causes of good and bad writing." It is packed with flashing metaphors, some obscure to the uninitiated, but significant when explained. It combines a bow to the ancient writers, advice to modern ones, definitions of the main types of literature, a series of cautions against different kinds of bad writing, and finally a lyrical account of the writer's creative processes, his difficulties, troubles, joys, and ideals. The Fang translation divides the text as follows: Preface; Preparation; Process; Words, Words, Words; Virtue; Diversity; The Poet's Aim; Genres; Multiple Aspects; Revision; Key Passages; Plagiarism; Purple Patches; Five Imperfections (In Vacuo, Discord, Novelty for Novelty's Sake, License, Insipidity); Variability; Masterpieces; The Poet's Despair; Inspiration; Coda: Encomium.

Lu Chi's principles are fairly flexible as compared with

---

that of E. R. Hughes, who adds an interesting comparison of Greek and Chinese ideas. This translation has been severely criticized by Achilles Fang, who provides a different one. Mr. Fang's is favored by the sinologists whom I have consulted on the subject. E. R. Hughes' version, entitled *The Art of Letters: Lu Chi's "Wen Fu,"* was published in the Bollingen Series (New York, Pantheon, 1951). It was reviewed at length by Achilles Fang in the *Harvard Journal of Asiatic Studies*, XIV (1951), pp. 615–636. In the same journal, pp. 527–566, Mr. Fang published his own version with the original Chinese text and extensive analytical footnotes. It is entitled "Rhymeprose on Literature: the Wen-Fu of Lu Chi (A.D. 261–303)." My summary here is based largely on the Fang translation.

some of the rigid rules of later Confucianism. He allows for many kinds of good writing. "Forms vary in a thousand ways; objects are not of one measure. [The Poet] may depart from the square and deviate from the compasses; for he is bent on exploring the shape and exhausting the reality. Hence, he who would dazzle the eyes makes much of the gorgeous; he who intends to convince the mind values cogency. If persuasion is your aim, do not be a stickler for details; when your discourse is lofty, you may be free and easy in your language." Different genres require different treatment. Lyric poetry traces emotions daintily; dirges are tense and mournful; admonitions are clear-cut and vigorous; eulogies are free and easy, rich and lush; memorials to the throne are quiet and penetrating, genteel and decorous; discourses are dazzling bright and extravagantly bizarre. Unbridled license is forbidden in all.

Inspiration ebbs and flows. At times, "The wind of thought burst from the heart; the stream of words rushes through the lips and teeth." At others, the emotions become sluggish; the poet is "as forlorn as a dead stump, as empty as the bed of a dry river." His reason, darkened, "is crouching lower and lower"; his thought must be "dragged out by force, wriggling and struggling." Then he makes many mistakes; he beats his empty breast and groans. In general, literary style serves as a prop for ideas; it contemplates the examples of the ancients and bequeaths patterns to the future.

Literary ideals somewhat like those of Lu Chi were stated more fully in a later classic of theory; that of Liu Hsieh on *The Literary Mind and the Carving of Dragons*.[81] Like

[81] Translated with an Introduction and Notes by Vincent Yu-chung Shih (New York, Columbia Univ. Press, 1959). This translation of the *Wên-hsin tiao-lung*, said to be the first into any modern language, was criticized by Professor J. R. Hightower in the *Harvard Journal of*

Aristotle's *Poetics*, it is explicitly devoted to literature, but treats that art so broadly as to have wide implications for art in general. Excessively ornate, elaborate carving is like overdecorated literature, too full of unnecessary curlicues and surface glitter. Many allusions are made to music and the visual arts.

This book is closer to being a general treatise on aesthetics than any other Chinese classic yet translated into English. It reviews and criticizes literary theories and critical opinions in China up to the author's time (A.D. 465–522) and discusses a long list of theoretical problems in a manner somewhat like that of Western critics in the Neo-classical period. Among the topics treated are these: the interpretation of poetry as disciplined emotional expression (p. 32), rules of prosody and harmony (39), types of poetry (45–154), style and nature (158), metaphor and allegory (195), literary flaws (216), the nourishing of artistic vitality and talent (222, 249), and the organization of language and ideas into unified forms (225).

This last topic, that of unity in variety, presents the essence of the classical ideal in art, aesthetics, ethics, and politics in every advanced civilization, East and West. It char-

---

Asiatic Studies, XXII, Dec. 1959. To the common reader, it seems to have much of value. Professor Hightower agrees that Liu Hsieh's book is "undoubtedly the most important Chinese treatise on literature and enormously influential on all subsequent Chinese writing about literature." Liu Hsieh's title, says Professor Hightower, means "A Serious and Elegant Treatise on . . . Literature." Like Lu Chi, he was interested "in the way the minds of great writers functioned." On dragon-carving, Mr. Hightower suggests this translation: "Literature has always employed something of the engraver's (or the embroiderer's) art to get its effects, and so I do not want my 'dragon-carving' to be taken as the ineffectual verbosity of a Tsou Shih." (pp. 284, 286). Professor Hightower has himself published many works in this field, including *Topics in Chinese Literature* (Cambridge, Mass., Harvard Univ. Press, 1953). This book discusses the poetic genres and the classic and popular styles, with biographical references.

acterizes the well-ordered state and the harmonious, rational personality. After each chapter, Liu Hsieh appends a short comment or summary. This one follows the chapter on "Organization":

> If a general principle underlies the different parts
>   of a piece,
> And feeling is rich and ordered;
> If it is well begun and well concluded,
> The branches well laid out and the leaves spread well,
> Then the piece will have an artistic harmony,
> All the loose threads will be gathered up
> And, like harmony in music,
> The sounds of the mind will blend perfectly.

Literature has developed, says Liu Hsieh, from the simple to the ornate and complex. (p. 233). In other words, it has evolved in some respects, as Plato also observed with distaste. As both perceived, such evolution does not imply progress or improvement. The Chinese writer was aware of another fact which Marx and Taine were to describe at length in the nineteenth century: that the literary forms and contents of each age express the spirit of the age, and that this in turn is affected by economic, social, moral, and political conditions. (p. 233f).

The Art of Chinese Poetry, by J.J.Y. Liu, a Chinese scholar now living in the West, analyzes that art in terms of verbal music as well as meanings and forms.[82] He also touches on the traditional aims and principles of poetry. There were four, he says: first the *didactic* (poetry as moral instruction and social comment); second, the *individualistic* (poetry as self-expression); third, the *technical* (poetry as a literary exercise for display of ability); and fourth, the *intuitionalist* (poetry as an embodiment of the poet's contemplation of the world and of his own mind).

---

[82] (London, Routledge and Kegan Paul, 1962).

This last conception arose under Ch'an-Zen Buddhist influence, its first important spokesman being Yen Yü in the thirteenth century. From this point of view, poetry aims to capture the spirit of life and nature in words. Later critics added that poetry was concerned with expression of emotion and reflection of the external scene. One must also catch the "spiritual essence" of the thing and achieve a personal style or flavor. (p. 85). In theory, the Zen Buddhists relied more on inspiration than on imitation of the classics. In practice, they have not been able to avoid a good deal of imitation.

Part Two

Interpretation and Evaluation

11. The subjective emphasis in Oriental aesthetics

In the Chinese conception of art, says Laurence Binyon, we note "a much greater stress laid on the subjective element than with us." [83] Sakanishi remarks that "The art of painting is to Kuo Hsi a manifestation of the artist's power to comprehend and express the spiritual reality of concrete natural objects... This the artist can express only at the cost of intense mental energy and severe mental discipline." [84] Oriental aesthetics thus pays much attention to the artist's inner attitudes and mental processes, with advice as to how he can best attain a state of mind which is favorable to creation. This he is to do with care, perhaps long before taking up the brush or other instrument of his craft. However, he does not necessarily form a clear conception in advance of the work to be produced.

Even Confucianism, though on the whole more extroverted than the other great Eastern religions, emphasized the ideal of inner harmony for the ruler as a model for his subjects and the state at large. This implied, not only harmony within the individual, but also that between the inner man and the outer world.

Traditional Far Eastern culture, especially as dominated by Hindu and Buddhist religion, was in many ways more introverted than Western, more concerned with psychic self-control in quest of certain ideal states of mind, such as

[83] *The Flight of the Dragon* (London, Wisdom of the East Series, 1927), p. 14.
[84] *Essay on Landscape Painting*, p. 23. *The Spirit of the Brush*, pp. 17f.

freedom from desire and sensuous imagery, the attainment of serenity and peace, and ultimately enlightenment on a transcendental level with escape from rebirth. Much of its detailed observation was of the inner world of the individual soul in various attitudes and levels of attainment. That Deity or Absolute Being is to be found within, as immanent in each individual soul, was a favorite theme of metaphysics and religious art.[85]

In their more extreme forms, both Hinduism and Buddhism preach a world-rejecting attitude, with the hope of complete release from the outer world of sensuous allure and illusion. The chief avenue of mental escape is inward, toward the "jewel in the heart of the lotus." In the West such an attitude in an individual is regarded as verging toward the psychotic; as "schizoid." Even in India, as Heinrich Zimmer points out, the world-rejecting tradition is not the only one. He traces it to "pre-Aryan, yogic" culture, and asserts that it has been persistently opposed by the "vigorous affirmation of the world of flux and time" in Vedic Brahmanism. The latter he calls a "dionysian affirmation of the dynamism of the phenomenal spectacle," and adds that it is more to be found in art than in philosophy.[86]

R. Mukerjee discerns an intermediate degree between these traditions. "In poetry," he says, "the most striking common note in all the Indian literatures is romantic fervor and passion and an exaggerated subjectivism, where these have freed themselves from the traditional mystical devotional pose and context." [87] Subjectivism can persist

[85] Cf. H. Zimmer, *Philosophies of India* (New York, Pantheon, 1951).

[86] *Philosophies of India*, pp. 596ff. This antithesis would not be accepted by all historians. I mention it as a controversial theory. The Dravidians may have been as vigorously affirmative as the Aryans.

[87] *The Culture and Art of India* (New York, Pantheon, 1951), p. 371.

in many forms and degrees apart from religious mysticism. An individual can achieve a moderate amount of inner self-control and mental harmony in either Eastern or Western culture without going to extremes of yogic world-rejection.

In the West, the training of an artist is often largely restricted to overt, external techniques, the use of materials and instruments. It is commonly felt that aesthetic aims and inner attitudes are personal matters which can be left to each artist; if not regulated, they will take care of themselves. In Oriental aesthetics, as in Plato's, the emphasis is more the other way around. Techniques and materials are not neglected, but neither are the mental and emotional parts of the artistic process.[88]

As to appreciation, we in the West again emphasize objective aspects. We ask students to learn about the history of art and how to distinguish the various styles. We ask them to notice carefully the lines and colors or the melodies and chords which are coming to us from "out there" in the work of art. We say little to the student about putting himself into the right state of mind to enjoy and sympathize with the work of art. Indian aestheticians put more emphasis on how the spectator of a drama can assume the appropriate mood; how he can gradually adopt an attitude of detachment from ordinary life and readiness to identify himself in imagination with some of the characters in the situation represented. They distinguish, as we have seen, a great variety of desirable qualities in aesthetic experience,

[88] Harold Rugg, psychologist and educator, contrasts the Eastern and Western roads to creativity, including Yoga, Zen, unconscious imagination, and mysticism in the East and West. *Imagination: an Inquiry into the Sources and Conditions that Stimulate Creativity* (New York, Harper and Row, 1963), pp. 158, 185. See also F. Spiegelberg, *Zen, Rocks, and Water*, with Introduction by Sir Herbert Read (New York, Pantheon, 1961). Illustrations from Chinese and Japanese drawing and poetry.

69

at which both artist and appreciator may aim. Many Western artists and aestheticians reject the idea that art should aim to produce any specific mood or emotional response in the observer.

In general, Western psychology has recently paid less and less attention to inner phenomena, in art and other kinds of experience. In quest of scientific accuracy, it has become increasingly behavioristic, devoted to observing and measuring human behavior toward the external world. This involves an increasing tendency to avoid introspective or autoperceptive methods. Western psychology on the whole is more concerned with interpersonal and social behavior than with the subjective aspects of individual personality. To some extent, it tends to regard an introspective, inwardly meditative attitude as "shut in" and unhealthy; as something not to be encouraged in the young, except perhaps as part of some established religious program. Psychoanalysis, which turns the spotlight inward to reveal a vast, complex domain of conscious, preconscious and unconscious psychic life, tries to open up that realm to the analyst's view and perhaps to describe it in a verbal or other objective medium. It aims at self-control through bringing more of the unconscious into the light of conscious awareness and perhaps into communication with the outside world.

Our Western tendency, in other words, is to objectify and externalize the inner life, directing more and more attention and interest on outer objects and thoughts about them. Eastern subjectivism, on the contrary, tends to turn attention inward and away from the world of sensory phenomena. The Western tendency invites interest and effort toward active dealing with other persons and the natural environment, but it does not, necessarily, develop one's inner resources. Many in the West are nervous or afraid when alone, and must "kill time" with artificial, often trivial, entertainments and amusements. The Western attitude has led us to control more and more of the outside world in our vicinity, and to improve our physical health. As a Westerner, I believe these values outweigh those of the opposite, Eastern tradition. But in every such choice, something is lost as well as gained. It is often well to ask whether both sets of values can be achieved to some extent. No one can deny that the subjective phases of artistic production and appreciation are of central importance, or that they are susceptible in some degree to self-observation, description, and control. Yet Western psychology and aesthetics now ignore them for the most part, or treat them in an oversimplified, cursory manner.

Let us not exaggerate the contrast between Eastern introversion and Western extroversion. It is a matter of degree, and important exceptions occur on both sides. Westernization has decreased the difference in recent years, especially in Japan and China. Even in ancient times, there were many different kinds of person in the East and in the West. Some were outward-looking and some inward-looking. Severe self-discipline of thoughts and feelings did not prevent the Eastern artist from careful attention to perfecting the external product or performance. It did not prevent the Buddhist, Zen, or Taoist recluse from observing nature and describing or picturing it. In the West there have always been some persons inclined to anxious searching of the soul. The Church provided monastic retreats for such individuals. Subjectivism has been a minor strain in Western art for centuries. Since the Romantic period, it has dominated much of our music and literature, especially in the meditative lyric and the stream-of-consciousness type of novel. During the last few years it has been increasingly influential in painting.

One of its characteristic manifestations is the desire for

self-expression by the individual artist—an aim which Oriental and medieval Christian religion would have rejected as egotistic.[89] The desire to express one's own personality does involve a special interest in oneself; in that which is to be expressed; in one's inner attitudes, desires, emotions, and perhaps frustrations. Here again the Western artist, however self-conscious, differs markedly from his traditional Eastern counterpart. The latter, in theory at least, sought to achieve inner peace, serenity, and oneness with nature. Many Western artists are more eager to display before the public their moods of anxiety, frustration, discontent, mockery, rejection, exclusion, and resentment toward the modern world. Such attitudes are at the opposite pole from the Confucian ideal of inner harmony and the Taoist one of contentment with the natural course of things. The Western artist may not try to change his psychic discords into harmonies by self-discipline; he may prefer to vent them impulsively and perhaps aggressively for what they are. Any attempt at achieving or expressing an inner harmony one did not spontaneously feel would seem to some as dishonest, unrealistic, out of keeping with the present disorder of the world. The classic moods of harmony, rational order, and happiness, as preached in both the Eastern and the Western traditions, are precisely what much recent Western art has been trying to avoid.

[89] *Cf.* Coomaraswamy, *The Transformation of Nature in Art*, pp. 23, 47. Joseph Campbell notes that "The pathos of self-expression, the romantic glorification of the individual genius and life agony of the suffering artist, the parade of the unique personality, and the cults of novelty, which have been the life breath of Occidental art and letters since the Renaissance, are altogether repulsive to the Oriental spirit." ("The Cultural Setting of Asian Art," p. 32). Self-effacement is the ideal role of the great individual in the Orient. "Not invention but a fresh statement of the already known is the aim."

Some Western educators in the arts, assuming that creativity is improved and stimulated by close cooperation, urge the artist or art student into more "togetherness" than he wants or needs. They ask him to join in collective projects and to work in large, well-equipped "art centers" close to other artists. Luxurious buildings are erected and equipped with every conceivable mechanism to "integrate" all the arts under one roof. Extremists frown upon any desire to be alone as "anti-social." The requirements of mass education add to this pressure.

Yet the persistent interest of many Western artists in Zen and other approaches emphasizing the intuitive approach, the inner quest for *satori* as a flash of sudden insight, reveal an undercurrent of vague dissatisfaction with Western methods. One motive and function of Ch'an in China and Zen in Japan, it is said, was to give release from the overly socialized, enveloping patterns of behavior prescribed by Confucianism.

On a purely empirical level and with no mystical implications, it may be that Western psychology could profit from closer attention to the inner phenomena of aesthetic and artistic experience. Art education, likewise, might profit from more effort to release and foster the inner life of the individual, at least by providing him with opportunities for undisturbed meditation and solitary work when he desired them.

This does not mean that Oriental attitudes and methods can be successfully transplanted to the West *in toto*. They are hard to detach from their native religious and cultural contexts. When imitated under very different circumstances, they often seem ridiculous; mere fads and affectations. Many mystical cults, such as theosophy, have been imported from East to West and acquired a certain following here; but they do not substantially influence modern

Western art and civilization. In its more religious phases, Oriental subjectivism goes to extremes which are unacceptable to most Western minds.

12. Some comparisons between Oriental and medieval European aesthetics

"A remarkable feature of Indian culture," says Arnold Bake in discussing Indian music,[90] "is its ability to integrate many different and seemingly divergent tendencies against the background of a unifying philosophical thought." Thus *The Ocean of Music,* a thirteenth-century Indian treatise, locates music within an all-embracing cosmogony and physiology of the human body. It also shows how good music "bestows liberation" to the soul and "breaks the cycle of birth, death, and rebirth." Once more we find the ideal of *moksha,* liberation from the endless cycle of transmigration, as the "unifying philosophical thought" which binds together the most diverse human activities. According to this ideal, the highest aim and function of each art is anagogic, to serve this "final and supreme aspiration of man." [91] Each does so in its own way. Sound rules the world of speech and also changes silent life-breath into sounds with beauty and meaning.

My own limited observation confirms Mr. Bake's remark about Indian culture. Many of the Indian writings on philosophy and aesthetics which have come to my attention, both ancient and modern, are far more comprehensive, thorough, and systematic than any I have found

[90] In E. Wellesz, *Ancient and Oriental Music* (London, 1957), p. 196.
[91] *Sources of Indian Tradition,* pp. 213, 276ff, on *Moksha* as the fourth and highest end of man.

from China or Japan. They show the will and ability to develop a certain aesthetic theory in great detail, relating it to a metaphysical world-view on the one hand, and to a considerable amount of empirical data on the other. They are not pure metaphysics or devoted (like Kant's *Critique of Aesthetic Judgment,* for example) largely to analyzing and interrelating highly abstract concepts. They often show the results of long, close professional observation and experience of art from the standpoints of artist, manager, and appreciator. Abhinavagupta is the outstanding example, and Seami in Japan is somewhat similar. The religious, metaphysical framework is always nearby in the background and occasionally brought into full view. This attitude toward art is somewhat like that of Theophilus (a near contemporary in Europe of Abhinavagupta, c. 1106 A.D.).[92] The Indian scholar combines the religious and philosophical with the practical and hedonistic attitudes, emphasizing each at different times, but not confusing them.

Indian civilization was somewhat analogous to medieval European in its hierarchical structure. In one case this developed as a rigid caste system; in the other, as a feudal system with a double, parallel hierarchy of church and state, from the lowest serf and monk to Holy Roman Emperor and Pope. The medieval hierarchy was more theoretical than actual, however, with endless conflict over which head should be supreme. In practice its hereditary class system was less rigid than the caste system; there were many ways to rise or fall. But in both cultures a hierarchical way of thinking and of organizing works of art was common. In Europe, the *Divine Comedy* is the great example. In India, one finds it everywhere—in the huge sculptural reliefs on

[92] *The Various Arts,* trans. by C. R. Dodwell (London, Nelson, 1961).

different levels over the surface of architecture, and in giving the highest god (as conceived by a particular religion) large size and central position. In India as in medieval Europe, the dominant value-system was hierarchical.

Dante arranges the vices and virtues in a hierarchy from the lowest hell to the highest heaven; Indian writers think of life as a series of levels from crude, animal-like sensuality to enlightenment, release, and union with the Absolute at the top. But Hindu and Buddhist cosmology does not conceive the hierarchy as fixed and eternal. In the grip of Maya (illusion) and the cycle of rebirths, it is rather to be symbolized by a wheel, as in some complex Tibetan Buddhist mandalas. Gods, men, and animals go perpetually up and down the scale unless and until they attain complete release from the wheel of existences.

The hierarchical conception pervades Indian aesthetics also in that (a) some kinds of art are more valuable than others in aiding this ascent and (b) some kinds of aesthetic experience are more advanced, spiritual, de-individualized, and universalized than others. On the highest level, awareness of the difference between subject and object disappears and no external, sensory stimulus is needed.

Some Indian art is devoted mainly to *Kama* (beauty and pleasure), which is a permissible but inferior end of man, while some is on a higher, more spiritual level, more valuable as an anagogic aid. Among the latter are the various diagrams (mandalas and yantras) which, in circular or other geometrical form, symbolize for Hinduism and Buddhism the "unity of a secluded and undiverted consciousness . . . reintegration to that Absolute Consciousness, entire and luminous, which Yoga causes to shine once more in the depths of our being." [93] According to Professor Tucci, the

[93] G. Tucci, *The Theory and Practice of the Mandala* (London,

best example of a Hinduist mandala is that called the Wheel of Sri—that is, of the divine power which is the motive force of the universe, shown in things which are of necessity. "Such mandalas are made by four isosceles triangles with the apices upwards, and by five others with the apices downwards... In the middle is a point, the mysterious matrix." The downward ones symbolize fulfilment; the others the return." [94] Everything here is geometrical design with little or no representation. These are instruments of the mind for contemplation and understanding both of self and cosmos. But much representational art contains this type of geometrical design, which Tucci describes as "an outer enclosure and one or more concentric circles which, in their turn, enclose the figure of a square cut by transversal lines." For example, the statue of dancing Siva Nataraja (symbolizing cosmic creation and destruction) is often surrounded by a circular flame. Many paintings show concentric circles of dancers, yogis, etc. [95] The symbolism of Hindu and Buddhist art is often extremely complex and metaphysical; hence comprehensible only to the initiate and erudite. A bare, geometrical yantra is not superior aesthetically, but functions on a higher spiritual plane than most representational art. Contemplation of the Crucifix possessed anagogic power for many Christian mystics, comparable to that of the mandala and yantra. [96]

Rider, 1961), p. 25. A. Daniélou, *Hindu Polytheism* (New York, Pantheon, 1964, Bollingen LXXIII), pp. 334–362.

[94] Pp. 46–47.

[95] *Cf.* Coomaraswamy, *Elements of Buddhist Iconography* (Cambridge, Mass., Harvard Univ. Press, 1935). Shah, *The Splendour That Was Ind*, plate LIV, Rasamandala. Krishna's dance with the cowgirls is often portrayed in circular form. See W. G. Archer, *The Loves of Krishna* (New York, Grove), pp. 74–75.

[96] On the kinship between Indian and medieval European metaphysics and aesthetics, see A. Coomaraswamy, *The Transformation of Nature in Art*, pp. 39f, 61f, in regard to Meister Eckhardt. Other

In Japan, Kūkai wrote of the treasures brought back from T'ang dynasty China, "The secret treasures of the *mantras* and the hidden mysteries of the *sūtras* and their commentaries cannot be transmitted without the aid of pictorial documents... Li Chên, with more than ten assistants, was ordered to paint the Garbh-dhatu and Vājrā-dhatu and other great mandalas." Elsewhere, he had this to say about the religious functions of art: "The esoteric doctrines are so profound as to defy their enunciation in writing. With the help of painting, however, their obscurities may be understood. The various attitudes and mudras of the holy images all have their source in Buddha's love, and one may attain Buddhahood at sight of them. Thus the secrets of the sutras and commentaries can be depicted in art, and the essential truths of the esoteric teaching are all set forth therein. Neither teachers nor students can dispense with it. Art is what reveals to us the state of perfection."

Sherman E. Lee points out a significant analogy between this and the Latin poem by Abbot Suger of St. Denis (1081–1151):

> Bright is the noble work; but, being nobly bright, the work
> Should brighten the minds, so that they may travel, through the true lights,
> To the True Light where Christ is the true door.

expressions of the mystical, spiritualistic view of Indian art are as follows: A. Coomaraswamy, "The Intellectual Operation in Indian Art," *Journal of the Indian Society of Oriental Art,* June 1935, pp. 1–12; "The Technique and Theory of Indian Painting," *Technical Studies in the Field of the Fine Arts,* Fogg Art Museum, Harvard, Cambridge, Mass., III, 2 (Oct. 1934), pp. 58–89; "One Hundred References to Indian Painting," *Artibus Asiae,* No. 1, 1930–32, pp. 41–57; "Further References...," *Ibid.,* pp. 126–129; "Abhasa," *Journal of the American Oriental Society,* LII, No. 3, pp. 208–220; N. C. Mehta, *Studies in Indian Painting* (Bombay, Taraporevala, 1926); J. de Marquette, "From Art to Spirituality," and other essays in *Art and Thought* (K. B. Iyer, ed.), in honor of A. K. Coomaraswamy (London, Luzac, 1947).

In what manner it be inherent in this world the golden
door defines:
The dull mind rises to truth through that which is material
And, in seeing this light, is resurrected from its former sub-
mersion.[97]

There are also important differences between Indian and
medieval European civilization, and these, too, expressed
themselves in art and aesthetics. Medieval art theory, as
exemplified in St. Augustine, was much preoccupied with
the evils of idolatry and sensual allure. Hindu art and aesthetics show little or no anxiety on these matters. Christian
philosophers were much concerned with the question
whether magnificent ornament, music, and ritual should be
prohibited or practiced in the service of religion. This did
not worry the Indian philosophers much. Anyone who
wanted a life of poverty could practice it as a monk or hermit in either India or Europe. Indian tradition conceived a
good life more in terms of its stages from infancy to old age.
Erotic and aesthetic enjoyments were right and suitable for
the young, married householder; asceticism and *moksha* for
old age. In both Indian and Europe, extreme asceticism including celibacy was not enjoined for all but was admired
and praised for those individually inclined to it.

Indian religion was frankly and exuberantly polytheis-
tic:[98] a trait which greatly stimulated artistic representation
and varied ritual. This was not inconsistent with a metaphysical monism in which individual gods were regarded as

[97] S. E. Lee, "The Secret Five," on the Shingon or "True Word" sect
of Buddhism in Japan. *Bulletin of the Cleveland Museum of Art*,
XLIX, No. 7 (Sept. 1962), p. 159. The passages on Kūkai are quoted
from W. R. B. Acker, *Some T'ang and Pre-T'ang Texts on Chinese
Painting* (Leiden, E. J. Brill, 1954), p. 262 and from Rynsaku Tsundo,
de Bary and Keene, *Sources of the Japanese Tradition*, p. 142. The
Suger lines are from E. Panofsky, *Abbot Suger* (Princeton, Princeton
Univ.), pp. 47, 49.

[98] On Hindu polytheism in general, see Daniélou, *op. cit.*

manifestations of Brahma or Vishnu. Christianity has been at least nominally monotheistic, but has evolved the artistic equivalent of a pantheon in the Trinity, Holy Family, and countless angels, saints, good spirits, and evil spirits. Christianity did not fear transmigration as Hinduism did; its goal was heaven and not escape from rebirth. (Plato and some Neo-Platonists believed in transmigration.) One should also note the relative brevity of the Christian era from its beginning to the present; its rapid succession of far-reaching social, political, intellectual, and artistic changes. It comprises a series of very different culture-patterns, each with its own artistic styles and aesthetic attitudes. The history of Indian civilization has been longer and more continuous and stable, though not completely so.

"The art of India is neither religious nor secular," says Stella Kramrisch.[99] She goes on to explain that these areas of life have never been "rent apart" as in the West. Every aspect of life is fitted into "a known hierarchy of values including the metaphysical. Every part has its own transcendental norm." Dr. Kramrisch then proceeds to explain Indian architecture and sculpture in terms of an elaborate, universal, established symbolism, comparable to that of a Gothic cathedral, but of longer standing. No part or mathematical proportion in the temple is accidental, she says. Even the materials are symbolic. "Brick, for instance, is the substance of the sacrificial altar, and therefore signifies the sacrifice itself." [100] Dr. Kramrisch's interpretation can be taken equally well to mean that Indian art is *all* religious, in that all of it, however secular on the surface, has a spiritualistic symbolism.

[99] *The Art of India Through the Ages* (London, 1955), p. 10.
[100] *Ibid.*, p. 16. *Cf.* Kramrisch, *The Hindu Temple* (Calcutta, 1946); *Indian Sculpture* (London, 1933); *Indian Sculpture in the Philadelphia Museum of Art* (Philadelphia, Univ. of Pennsylvania, 1960).

Stella Kramrisch, Paul Mus, Alice Boner,[101] and other Orientalists have elaborately explained the geometrical proportions of Hindu architecture and sculpture, as well as the intricate religious symbolism of the forms thus planned and built. Miss Kramrisch emphasizes the square as the leading architectural symbol—that of the extended world in its order. "It has precedence over the circle of time." Squares, circles, pyramids, and other forms are combined in definite proportions to make the complex ground-plan and superstructure of the Hindu temple.

In diagramming the compositional patterns of Hindu sculpture, Miss Boner emphasizes the circular field around a central point and its subdivision by chords and diameters. "Viewed in the light of man's adventure," she writes, "the central point would stand for the Atman, and the circle would encompass the entire development of his existence and his spiritual life. Movements tending away from the center would represent the entanglement in the world of Maya, the way of egotistic worldly life, . . . while movements tending from the periphery towards the center would represent the way of return to the source of Being." (p. 29f). The figural compositions, she adds, refer to "timeless mysteries" and "transcendent reality" in anthropomorphic garb.

The column, stupa, and temple mountain, says Benjamin Rowland, suggested in their form the appearance of the heavens of the gods or of the cosmos.[102] They were intended to make other-worldly things more accessible through magic, and to give the builder power over what he represented. The fundamental architectural forms are based on

[101] *Principles of Composition in Hindu Sculpture, Cave Temple Period* (Leiden, Brill, 1962).

[102] "The World's Image in Indian Architecture," *Journal of the Royal Society of Arts,* CXII, No. 5099 (Oct. 1964), pp. 795–807.

the idea of a world axis; sometimes as a pillar separating heaven and earth. The basic cosmic diagram points to the zenith and extends its arms to the cardinal points. The Buddhist stupas contained vestiges of their early function as symbols of the world ruler. The cupola is the cosmic egg of Brahma's creation, floating on the ocean of chaos. Barabudur, in Java, is the last and most complex magic symbol of the cosmos in architecture. It shows the world mountain enclosed in the dome of the sky, and functions as a mandala or magic diagram of the cosmic system. The reliefs of its successive terraces, Professor Rowland shows, begin with life in the world of desire and go from the early incarnations of the mortal Buddha to the careers of the greatest Mahayana Bodhisattvas. The world of form is shown in the closed squares of the lower terraces; the formless world in the unbounded space of the round platforms on the top. The Buddhist world axis is comparable to the cosmic tree of other ancient religions, symbolizing in various ways the all-embracing cosmic person.

In general, the symbolic iconography of Hindu and Buddhist art has been known to Western Orientalists for several decades. What is comparatively new to them (and to most Eastern scholars) is the detailed iconometry and the complex geometrical forms, contained in Indian art, which convey the traditional meanings. Recent investigators have utilized two kinds of evidence: (1) actual measurements and diagrams of ground-plans, elevations, rooms, sculptural layouts, etc., and (2) references to the classical Sanskrit writings. Geometrical design and mystic symbolism were integral parts of ancient Hindu art and aesthetics. Without reference to them, the art of ancient India cannot be thoroughly understood today.

In this respect there is a kinship between Indian aesthetics and the Pythagorean strain in Western aesthetics, some of which survived in Neo-Platonic and medieval mysticism. But mathematics in the West did not develop far in subjection to religious symbolism. It largely freed itself from these in Hellenistic times and developed thereafter as a rationalistic, secular science, capable of application to architecture, surveying, and other practical technology without mystic implications.

It is possible to accept the mystical interpretation of Hindu art as true in a limited sense, without believing in the religious or metaphysical world-view it implies. One can agree that the symbolic forms and meanings described by Coomaraswamy, Kramrisch, and others are actual cultural phenomena. At the same time one can reject the belief, apparently held by these writers, that the ideas symbolized refer to transcendental, divinely established truths.

Contemporary aestheticians differ in India as in the West. P. J. Chaudhury denies the usual view that traditional aesthetics is governed by metaphysics in India. It is the other way around, he thinks.[103] Indian conceptions of the world emphasize its illusory nature as divine, imaginative re-creation; as God's work of art.

A. L. Basham goes farther in rejecting the strongly religious interpretation of Indian art which is accepted by most present critics and historians.[104] He maintains that writers such as Coomaraswamy have read Buddhist and Vedantist ideas into it as "sermons in stone on the oneness of all things in the Universal Spirit," whereas "it is the full and active life of the times which is chiefly reflected in the art of ancient India." There is an intense vitality in it, he adds, "which remind us rather of this world than the next." Especially in visual art, "the usual inspiration is not so

[103] "Aesthetical Metaphysics," *The Visvabharati Quarterly*, XXII, No. 2 (Autumn 1956), p. 95.
[104] *The Wonder That Was India* (London, Sidgwick & Jackson, 1954), pp. 346f.

much a ceaseless quest for the Absolute as a delight in the world as the artist found it, a sensual vitality, and a feeling of growth and movement as regular and organic as the growth of living things upon the earth." The visual art, Mr. Basham adds, is chiefly the work of secular craftsmen, whereas the religious literature came from men with a religious vocation: Brahmins, monks, and ascetics. In his own well-informed history of Indian culture, he deals objectively with both religion and the arts but detaches them somewhat, explaining each in its own right without overemphasizing the religious aspects.

Aubrey Menen, a contemporary Indian fiction-writer, prefaces his modern version of the *Ramayana* with some caustic remarks on the influence of Brahmins on Indian civilization. Twenty-five centuries ago, he says, the Brahmins were courtiers and top dogs. They made the laws, taught the ignorant, dictated morals, controlled the temples, and terrified the king. They had not yet become a rigid and hereditary caste. They accused Valmiki, author of the *Ramayana*, of killing a Brahmin, which is doubtful. "Unfortunately, generations of Brahmins have re-written his poem so that in parts it says the opposite of what Valmiki plainly intended." [105]

13. Universal symbolism in Indian and medieval European art. Opposing interpretations

We have seen that Indian art and aesthetics are analogous to medieval European in their persistent emphasis on mystic symbolism. In the West, this approach to art, the Bible, and the world was developed by Origen, Clement of Alexandria,

[105] *The Ramayana* (New York, Scribner's, 1954), p. 4.

and St. Augustine,[106] the last of whom wrote theoretically on music and other arts. The belief in universal symbolism and the tendency of writers to find mystic meanings throughout nature and art prevailed through St. Thomas and Dante, declining after the Council of Trent. Even in the Gothic period, however, the interest in nature and human nature for their own sake was reviving and competing successfully with the allegorical tradition. The latter declined more and more as naturalism and classicism grew in the Renaissance and Baroque periods. A similar change took place in Chinese and Japanese art in recent centuries, with symbolism becoming more and more perfunctory and often merely amusing or decorative, as in the common symbols of longevity and prosperity on ceramics and textiles. It is still taken much more seriously in the study of Indian art.

Mr. Menen is not the only one to suggest that the present interpretation of Indian art is something largely invented by the Brahmin caste, hereditary custodians of religion, education, and scholarship. That it permeated their philosophic writings, including those on aesthetics, does not necessarily mean that it was taken quite as seriously by the rest of the population, including artists and members of other castes. In medieval Europe while the belief in universal symbolism was at its height, a great many artists and craftsmen seem to have paid little attention to the intricate burden of theological meanings which clerical commentators laid upon their works. In India, too, it may be that the extremely religious interpretation of art is mainly the ex-

[106] St. Augustine, *On Christian Doctrine*, D. W. Robertson, trans. (New York, 1958). See also the *Confessions* and *On Music*. Cf. Dante, "Letter to Can Grande della Scala," on the symbolism of the *Divine Comedy*. The European theory of universal symbolism can be traced in part to Platonism, with its doctrine of the eternal Ideas, and even farther back to the Pythagorean and other mystery cults.

85

pression of the traditional Brahmin ideology, rather than that of India as a whole. Most of the philosophic writers have been Brahmins or directly under their influence. It is often hard to decide whether a certain work or type of art has a certain symbolic meaning. One's approach to it depends on one's whole philosophic world-view. Indian and medieval Christian mystics believed in universal symbolism on a transcendental basis: that certain things or images in the phenomenal world (such as a wheel or a lion) have higher, spiritual meanings through the very nature of the universe and of divine will. Man can discover some of them. An artist, consciously or not, can express them in his art through divine or cosmic inspiration. Such meanings in art may be understood only by the few enlightened minds; they are not determined by general cultural usage. Other persons, looking at the same work of art, might not grasp them even by extended study.

One cannot be sure that a work of art has no allegorical meaning by merely observing it. Sometimes the symbolism of a certain image is explained in the work of art itself, as in some parts of the Christian *Apocalypse*. ("The seven stars are the angels of the seven churches.") At other times it is left obscure or cryptic. Even the meaning of so common a thing as a national flag can usually not be inferred by merely looking at it; one must have some outside information as to what country it stands for. One might watch *The Little Clay Cart* many times without knowing whether it has a deeper meaning that that which is explicit in the text. The same is true of much Indian sculpture and painting. Some is obviously religious, some apparently not.

Philosophic naturalism rejects the basic theory of universal symbolism. Nothing has a symbolic meaning by the nature of things or by divine will. All symbolic meanings are attributed by humans and more or less enduringly at-

PLATE VI. *Krishna Playing His Flute*. India, Rajput,
Rajasthan, Bundi, 19th century. (The Cleveland Museum
of Art, Gift of Mr. and Mrs. Arthur D. Brooks).

PLATE VII. *Head of a Bodhisattva*. Chinese, Sung Dynasty, 12th century, wood. (The Cleveland Museum of Art).

tached to images by cultural usage; sometimes by a whole social group and sometimes by a small élite of initiates. The question whether a certain image or work of art has or does not have a certain meaning is partly one of the intentions of the artist and those who ordered and used it when it was first made. It has or had that meaning insofar as that usage was culturally established, and is still practiced.

A certain work or type of art—e.g., poems and paintings of the loves of Krishna—is often understood in different ways as time goes on. Different stories and attributes are attached to the same divine or heroic personage. A certain story, historic or fictitious, may first be told in purely human terms, or with a primitive symbolism based on magic and religious animism. It is well known that many ancient myths were attempts to explain the cause and origin of natural phenomena such as rain and sunshine, summer and winter, the fertility of crops and herds. They were used in magico-religious rituals to control the phenomena concerned. Stories and visual images with a strongly sexual emphasis are often of this type. Krishna's flute is a phallic symbol, but that is not its only meaning. It also symbolizes the spiritual power of music. As tastes and manners became more refined and metaphysical thinking developed, the original symbolism often came to seem too crude, obscene, or violent. Poets, philosophers, and priests tried to substitute more abstract, religious interpretations. According to the *Krishna Upanishad*, the god Rudra was Krishna's flute. In the *Gopāla-pūrvatāpini Upanishad* he is called the protector of all sacred utterances (symbolized as cows) and the instigator of all forms of knowledge (symbolized as cowherdesses).[107]

Which of these interpretations is the true one? From the naturalistic standpoint, none of them is *the* true, deeper

[107] Daniélou, *op. cit.*, pp. 175–6.

meaning in any transcendental sense. All of them are correct as accounts of cultural phenomena; of how certain people understood an image at certain times and places. If the metaphysical interpretation won a large, authoritative usage for long periods, it deserves to be emphasized in modern histories of art and iconology. But it is not necessarily more true, or on a higher plane, than a purely secular, literal interpretation, or one in terms of primitive seasonal mythology. Modern spiritualists have every right to prefer the mystical interpretation, but no right to assert that it is *the* correct one by the ultimate nature of things.

Problematic in this respect are the amorous adventures of Zeus in Greek mythology and of Jupiter and Bacchus in Roman. When a cow or bull is involved, as in the stories of Io and Europa, a pastoral origin of the myth is suggested. The same is true of Krishna and the cowgirls.

W. H. Archer[108] recounts in detail the changing conception of Krishna and his deeds in India from the tenth to the twelfth century. From being a warrior prince in the *Bhagavata Purana,* he changes to the cowherd lover in the *Gita Govinda (Song of the Cowherd)* by Jayadeva. His adulterous romance with the married cowgirl, Radha, "is to serve as a sublime allegory expressing and affirming the love of God for the soul." "Radha's sexual passion for Krishna," says Mr. Archer, "symbolized the soul's intense longing, and her willingness to commit adultery expressed the utter priority which must be accorded to love for God." In addition, the story was a fulfilment of human desires for romance, which were increasingly difficult under growing marital restriction. "In removing the clothes of the cowgirls and requiring them to come before him naked, he was demonstrating the innocent purity with which the soul

---

[108] *The Loves of Krishna,* Ch. V, esp. pp. 72–75. *Cf.* M. S. Randhawa, *Kangra Paintings on Love* (New Delhi, National Museum, 1962).

should wait on God." In neglecting Radha, he was proving "the power of God to love every soul irrespective of its character and status." The circular dance proved "how God is available to all," and his departure from Radha symbolized "the dark night of the soul."

Mr. Archer invites comparison of the tale as so interpreted with the works of St. John of the Cross, sixteenth-century Spanish mystical poet, who also expresses "the longing of the soul for God . . . in terms of sexual imagery." Here the allegoric intention of the artist is clear and much of the symbolism explicit in the text. One could hardly limit his meanings to the purely human, literal ones.

A somewhat different situation exists in regard to "The Song of Songs," in the Hebrew *Old Testament*. Some scholars, not bound by any official interpretation, now find reason to believe that this was originally a group of secular songs of love and wedding. It is frankly erotic and physical in its imagery. Yet it was traditionally attributed to Solomon, who was regarded as a model of wisdom and piety; hence an allegorical interpretation seemed necessary if the songs were to be included in the canon. The Hebrews interpreted the songs as celebrating the love of Yahweh for Israel; Yahweh as bridegroom, Israel as bride. "The Christian Church," says Professor J. A. Bewer,[109] "accepted the allegorical interpretation, but regarded Christ as the bridegroom and the Church or the soul as the bride." The Council of Trent discouraged excessive allegorizing, but the Authorized Version of 1611 (King James Version) still includes allegorical chapter-headings for "The Song of Songs." For Chapter I, the heading begins, "The church's

[109] *The Literature of the Old Testament* (New York, Columbia Univ. Press, 1940), pp. 391–393. *Cf.* R. G. Moulton, *The Modern Reader's Bible* (New York, Macmillan, 1925), pp. 1448ff.

love unto Christ." A later one is "The church having a taste of Christ's love is sick of love."

Histories of culture and of world literature must certainly report that these various allegorical interpretations were made by certain groups and widely accepted for a time. These meanings now form recognized parts of the traditional iconology of "The Song of Songs." But objective historians and aestheticians are under no obligation to believe that such allegories are the true, correct ones, or that persons on a high mental level are sure to believe them. To believe them is an act of religious faith, not of science or scholarship. The more we learn about the history of "The Song of Songs," the more such allegories may come to seem far-fetched, gratuitous, and unwarranted. From an aesthetic standpoint, they seem to many readers as disagreeable irrelevancies, interfering with direct enjoyment of the work of art. If anyone prefers to disregard them and read "The Song of Songs" in its original sense as a set of secular love-songs, he has every right to do so. He need not feel that he is thereby entering a lower plane of aesthetic appreciation.

The same is true of "Krishna and the Cowgirls," in poetry and painting. Here many Western admirers of Indian art will prefer to ignore the metaphysics, if possible. The sensuous, narrative, and human aspects are quite enough to reward intensive study. Some elements of religious symbolism form an integral part of Indian art and cannot be ignored without missing important values. Much of this refers to related myths and primitive cosmology, such as the "Churning of the Milky Ocean," [110] which are themselves colorful narratives. The meanings they add are welcome as pure fantasy, apart from any question of be-

[110] H. Zimmer, *Myths and Symbols in Indian Art and Civilization* (Pantheon, 1946), p. 105.

lief. But it is also possible to think that Indian philosophers have carried abstract, metaphysical allegory much too far in interpreting Indian art, and in expecting the world to believe in its truth. Perhaps Indian culture could profit from a new Council of Trent, to discourage excessive allegory.

Aesthetics as an objective, world-wide science is under no obligation to emphasize the symbolic, religious aspects of Indian art as much as its devoutly mystical interpreters have done. Some other aspects of Indian art and aesthetics, especially the more empirical and naturalistic, may be more valuable as well as more acceptable to the West.

14. Chinese and Japanese as compared with Indian aesthetics

In China and Japan, the Taoist and Buddhist traditions recognized a supernatural element in art and a transcendental level of aesthetic experience. But they did not develop these ideas theoretically as far as the Indians did.[111] Confucianism persistently emphasized the worldly, humanistic, secular side of life, and influenced both art and aesthetics accordingly. Says Wing-tsit Chan: "The influence of supernatural forces over man is completely ruled out by Hsün Tzu. What he called spirit is but cosmic change and evolution." [112]

[111] "When Buddhism in China became Chinese Buddhism, evolving as Zen, the practical this-worldliness of Chinese thinking modified the other-worldliness of Indian Buddhism and made it more acceptable to the themes of Chinese thought." (Mai-mai Sze, *The Tao of Painting,* p. 22.)

[112] *Source Book in Chinese Philosophy* (Princeton, 1963), p. 121. Mencius represented the more spiritualistic tendency in Confucianism. (p. 115). Hsün Tzu's attitude was widespread but not universal in later Confucianism.

Chinese civilization, says James Cahill,[113] resembles that of the West in being "a humanistic civilization repeatedly beset by doubts about the validity of the humanistic ideal." At a relatively early stage it developed "an aesthetic theory according to which painting serves to express the thought and feeling of the individual man," and this could have occurred only in a humanistic context. As contrasted with the anonymous artisan of traditional societies who suppressed his own personality, the Chinese was deeply concerned with "how to build a style into a personal instrument of expression." He sought to balance objective description and subjective content while endowing pictorial form with humane content. Ch'an Buddhism, in the Five Dynasties and Sung periods, denied the value of orthodox Buddhist rituals, deities, scriptures, and holy images in favor of individual enlightenment. This had to be attained through intuitive, not rational methods. Some Ch'an masters are pictured as burning images of Buddha and tearing up the sacred scriptures. (This invites comparison with the Byzantine iconoclast movement, which was partly a protest against supposed idolatry.)

Perhaps the most striking contrast between Chinese and Indian writings on aesthetics is the brevity of the former. This is true of both ancient and modern times. The Chinese and Japanese writings are, as a rule, short and limited in scope. They are literary and poetic rather than religious or metaphysical. Many are apparently casual, spontaneous, unexplained and obscure. Their authors were content with a few penetrating observations, suggestive but cryptic metaphors, maxims, and quick, arbitrary appraisals.

Metaphysics was not developed in China or Japan to the massive, complex proportions it assumed in India. Hence there was less temptation to base one's aesthetic theories

[113] Cahill, *Chinese Painting*, Introduction, pp. 47, 52.

92

upon it. The Chinese and Japanese thinkers were, on the whole, more concerned with ethics, politics, history, decorum, and the civilized enjoyment of life on this earth in harmony with nature and heavenly principles. Art and aesthetics grew up mostly within this framework. The Taoist-Buddhist tradition was more inclined to mystic supernaturalism than the Confucian, but it was opposed to large-scale, rational systems of thought. Many of its leaders wrote nothing, expressing themselves by significant actions and inactions. Others uttered short, cryptic phrases and epigrams; apparent nonsense which turned out to have a hidden meaning, but not necessarily a religious one.[114] Recently, as in the writings of Dr. Suzuki, there has been a strong effort to explain Ch'an Zen as a systematic, rational theory.

One persistent factor in Chinese metaphysical thinking, the Yin-Yang (feminine-masculine, passive-active) dualism, was comparatively limited and unproductive as a starting-point for comprehensive explanations of the world. It was more directly relevant to human life and to representations of life in art. The Yin-Yang dualism found symbolic expression in all forms of art in China and Japan; even in flower arrangement.

Another significant pair of metaphysical concepts, especially in later Confucianism, was that of *ch'i* (material force, matter) and *li* (principle). The latter is also explained as the eternal laws which give identity to individual objects and determine the changes they undergo. Since any object contains principle, there is some value in studying it. This idea may have been extended to cover the painter's

[114] See, for example, Paul Reps' compilation of Zen and pre-Zen writings called *Zen Flesh, Zen Bones* (Garden City, N. Y., Doubleday, 1961).

way of studying objects, including humble and ignoble ones.[115]

We must not suppose that the Chinese mind was incapable of extended, systematic reasoning when a sufficient motive existed. This was found more in empirical science and technology than in metaphysics. We are now discovering that the ancient Chinese had much more science and technology than has been supposed.[116] The importance given to political administration and the need for selecting capable men led, not only to the examination system, but to such books as Liu Shao's *Jen wu chih* (c. 245 A.D.).[117] This is a treatise on psychology and its applications, described by the translator as "consistent, thorough, and systematic." "It organized ancient ideas on the psychology of public life into an articulated whole." It stated definite hypotheses and laws, and applied them in ways that would never have occurred to Confucius. (p. 4). It classified types of personality and ability, including that of the literary man. (pp. 106, 109). Here was an empirical basis for a study of the psychology of artists in different media which was, so far as I know, never followed up.

Fung Yu-lan, contemporary historian of Chinese philosophy, acknowledges that the briefness and disconnectedness of Chinese philosophic writings are an obstacle to Western students.[118] In the *Analects* "there is hardly any

[115] On different conceptions of *ch'i*, *li*, and their interrelations, see W. T. Chan, *Source Book*, pp. 495ff, 547; de Bary (ed.), *Sources of Chinese Tradition*, pp. 510f, 536f.

[116] On their physical sciences, see Joseph Needham, *Science and Civilization in China* (Cambridge, Cambridge Univ. Press, 1954 *et seq.*).

[117] Trans. by J. K. Shryock as *The Study of Human Abilities* (New Haven, Conn., American Oriental Society, 1937).

[118] *A Short History of Chinese Philosophy* (New York, Macmillan, 1948), pp. 11ff. On the other hand, James Cahill speaks of "the vast and orderly structure of the Neo-Confucian cosmology" erected by the

connection between one paragraph and the next." Philosophy is expressed in "aphorisms, apothegms, allusions, and illustrations" in Lao-Tzu, Chuang-Tzu, Mencius, and Hsün Tzu. This is due in part, he says, to the fact that philosophy was not a profession; hence there were no formal philosophical works. That fact itself seems to need explanation. But it is significant that the limitations of Chinese philosophy were somewhat voluntary; not due to mere neglect or inability.

"Suggestiveness," Professor Fung continues, "is the ideal of all Chinese art, whether it be poetry, painting, or anything else." What the poet wants to communicate is often not what he says but what he does not say. One must read between the lines. In poetry, "The number of words is limited, but the ideas it suggests are limitless." It would be better to talk without words if one could get the ideas otherwise. The *Tao* "cannot be told, but only suggested." (Here we feel the touch of Taoist mysticism and of mystics everywhere: truly great thoughts are ineffable.)

Without going to extremes, one can readily acknowledge the values of suggestive, terse, economical expression and indirect, even cryptic, allusion in art. These are qualities sought by some Western artists also, but more persistently in Chinese and Japanese art, as in the "flung ink" drawings and the Haiku (short lyrics). Modern philosophy and art in the West (up to the present century at least) have striven rather for clarity and complex organization, sufficient to develop a theme or thesis to maturity. Among the ancient predecessors of philosophy in Babylonian, Hebrew, and early Greek culture, we find "wisdom literature" in short, pithy maxims, proverbs, and aphorisms, but these did not satisfy the growing philosophic appetite

---

Sung philosophers. Further translation may reveal a more systematic type of Chinese philosophy than we now possess.

of the West. Theoretical knowledge, in philosophy or aesthetics, cannot grow very far while limited to unconnected snatches of thought.

The greater philosophic development of Indian aesthetics is no unmixed blessing for most Western readers, however; certainly not for the naturalistic humanist. For him a great deal of the philosophy involved is unconvincing and tedious; an obsolete relic of medieval thinking which obscures the elements of humanistic value attached to it. Most of it is concerned with the relations between the individual self (Atman) and the Absolute Brahman or Supreme Being: a problem which (in the opinion of naturalists) is purely fictitious. The same can be said of the chief ethical problem of both Hinduism and Buddhism: how to achieve release from the cycle of rebirths. From the standpoint of Western and Carvaka naturalism, it is based on the purely fictitious assumption that rebirths occur.[119]

15. Social and cultural backgrounds of Oriental aesthetics. Classicism and conservatism

It was mentioned above that "aesthetics," in the modern sense as an organized branch of philosophy or science, did not exist in the ancient world, East or West. As such, it plays no part in cultural history until the nineteenth century. But its ancestors are to be found scattered through ancient and medieval writings on many subjects, especially in the form of general comments on art, artists, and related types of activity and experience. These are mostly vague, dogmatic, and unorganized; mere personal expressions of taste and preference, myths about the origins of art and

[119] Cf. Sources of Indian Tradition, pp. 300ff, 306.

beauty, or assertions as to what art ought to do and be. As a people develops intellectually, it may produce more systematic essays on certain arts. These early kinds of thinking and writing about art play a part in cultural history. In a broad sense, they can all be classed as aesthetics. I will briefly indicate some of their relations with other factors and processes in the history of civilized peoples.

We are now accustomed to the hypothesis—overworked by the Marxists but accepted in some degree by all historians—that social factors influence ideas and expression in every field, including art, religion, and philosophy. Attempts to explain the history of styles in any art lead one to consider other cultural processes, to see what correlation may exist among them. To what extent are style trends influenced by socio-economic changes, and vice versa? The study of Oriental art along these lines has hardly begun. Even less attention has been given, outside the Marxist sphere of influence, to the causal relations between social factors and aesthetic theories. Social conditions influence theories of art and vice versa. The arts, and theories of what art should do and be, have exerted a considerable influence on Indian thought and social action.

Mukerjee, whom I have quoted above as a philosopher and sociologist, summarizes the interrelation of factors in India thus: "The state, politics, and conquest are far less significant in India than metaphysics, religion, myth, and art as factors in social integration. There are hardly any people in the world who have been ruled so little by political occurrences . . . and so much by metaphysical and religious movements." [120] This is doubtless true. But it is also true that, in India as elsewhere, social factors have influenced metaphysics, religion, and art.

The art and aesthetics of a people express its different

[120] *The Culture and Art of India* (New York, 1959), p. 9.

value-systems, especially those of dominant groups therein —those which have the power to enjoy and profit from the arts and also to judge and influence them. Works of art and the opinions of influential people about them have the power to change the current value-system—tastes, desires, and standards of evaluation.

In a modern urban democracy much popular art is produced, appealing to all ages, classes of society, and types of personality. Some art is addressed especially to men, some to women, some to children of various ages; some to adults with little education. In the ancient aristocracies, folk art was largely unwritten; so were the opinions, if any, which common people expressed about art. We tend to conceive the arts of an ancient people, such as the Indians, largely in terms of the magnificent, complex, durable palaces, temples, statues, poems, and plays which have come down to us, as well as the kinds of music and drama which are performed in urban environments. These are the works which are featured in art museums and histories of art. They appealed to the interests and tastes of a dominant nobility and priesthood, or in later times to a wealthy merchant class, even though the lower classes might also see and enjoy those placed on public view. We often assume that these are the only works of art worth studying, and form our conception of the culture as a whole on the basis of these selected works. But they are only a part—sometimes a very small part—of the art produced by the group as a whole. Other kinds are produced by provincial artists or by minority cultures such as the Todas in India or the Ainu in Japan. However inferior in quality (and they are not always so) they are significant for an understanding of the whole culture and its history. Some of them are not mere poor imitations of élite art; they may be radically different, as in the music and folklore of American Negroes. Selected elements of folk art tend to work their way upward into the art of upper, educated classes, while those of élite art work downward.

Much the same can be said of ancient aesthetics; that is, of early attitudes toward the arts and theories about their nature, origin, and functions. Nearly all the philosophic theorizing about art in early civilizations was done by members of the priestly or educated noble class or by scribes under their direction who knew the art of writing. In India these were mostly Brahmins; in China, scholars educated in the Confucian classics. What such men approved and liked in art was likely to be that which conformed with their principles; that which tended to praise and glorify the accepted gods and rulers, and thus to reinforce the established social and cultural system. On the whole, it would be art which served the *status quo*, except where the *status quo* included some innovations which they did not approve. In that case, conservative taste might call as Plato did for a return to the simpler, morally preferable arts and customs which (supposedly) had existed in the good old days.

In comparing the arts of a certain culture and period with the aesthetic theories of that time and place, one is often puzzled by the divergence between them. Sometimes they seem quite inconsistent; the art violates or ignores the contemporary principles of art. This is a complex problem, deserving careful study. Many factors tend to dislocate art from theories of art, and often to make aesthetic theory lag behind. Art may revolt from established principles of the age, as in the time of Akhnaten. Centuries may elapse before the philosophers come around to accepting and approving artistic innovations. One contributing factor is that artists and philosophers tend to be different kinds of person: the former more sensuous, imag-

99

inative, and overtly active; the latter more intellectual and critical. Also, they sometimes come from different social and educational levels, as in India, where the educated intellectuals were mostly Brahmins.

But an apparent gulf between art and theory can be bridged over by theory in various ways. Joseph Campbell points out that "the usual point of view of the spiritual literature of the Orient is that of a monk or ascetic striving for the stilled, composed state (*samadhi*); that of the arts is rather rapture at the play of forms." [121] Hence, he says, it is hard to recognize in the voluptuous figures of Indian art "any connection with the purity and austerity of Indian Vedantic and Buddhist thought." However, Mr. Campbell maintains, all the forms of art and experience are (to Oriental metaphysics) "but inflections of the one form that we should see if our minds came to rest" (as through Yoga). The One is immanent, transcendent, and ubiquitous.

In Western as well as Eastern aesthetics, the influential classics which are emphasized in histories and courses on the subject are mostly writings which have been selected by conservative scholars in a long series of past generations. What we translate and publish in one edition after another and include in anthologies is mostly that which has satisfied the dominant groups in past ages. What is presented as Greek or Roman, Indian or Chinese traditional aesthetics does not represent all the main, conflicting views of artists and scholars in those ages, but only a few approved by the later scholars and officials who had control of publication, history-writing, and teaching. Not until the revolutionary writings of British and French liberals in the eighteenth century, and the Romantic movement which ensued, did the unorthodox, radical, individualistic theo-

[121] "The Cultural Setting of Asian Art," *College Art Journal* (Fall 1958), p. 25.

ries of art get a fair hearing. For example, Victor Hugo in his famous Preface to *Cromwell* made it clear that art, in modern times, included not only classical beauty but what he called the "grotesque"—the ugly but characteristic, the weird, fantastic, clownish and terrifying, sick and healthy, good and evil products of human imagination. Goethe said much the same thing, but Western aesthetics has not yet fully assimilated these insights, based on the actual achievements of art. In both East and West, the most influential aestheticians have too often ignored the major trends in art or blindly condemned them on *a priori* grounds. Modern liberals are now more used to the idea that opposing views should be fairly presented in philosophy, art, and aesthetics, but it is too late to rescue the lost, unorthodox views of the ancient and medieval worlds in West or East.

As to what unorthodox views were expressed, we can only conjecture. In the West, we know that practically all the writings of Epicurus and his early followers, as well as those of previous naturalists such as Democritus, are lost or destroyed. The ideas of Protagoras and other leading Sophists in Socrates' time are caricatured in Plato's dialogues, for easy refutation. Only a little remains of Aristotle's naturalistic aesthetics. The Epicureans, as chief opponents of mystic spiritualism, flourished throughout the Roman Empire until the Christian era. Among them, Lucretius and Horace wrote on art history and aesthetics and some of their writings have survived. But the influence of Plato, the mystic Neo-Platonists, and the modern spiritualistic philosophy derived from them, has overshadowed all the rest until recent times. Now there exists, in the Communist countries, a different kind of selection. The Marxist writings on aesthetics of Engels, Lenin, and others have become the new orthodoxy and are emphasized to the neglect of other traditions.

Most of the writings on aesthetics which have been preserved and venerated through the ages are conservative and classicist. Platonists and Confucianists praise and recommend ideals of social unity and order at the expense of individual freedom; they emphasize harmony, fulfillment of one's allotted tasks in life, obedience to rulers, faithful performance of established rituals, and the like. The only art to be encouraged is that which tends to glorify and reinforce this ideal conception of the state, to which individual liberty is subordinated. It must be simple, stately, joyous, invigorating, and must represent lofty types of character—gods, wise rulers, heroes, loyal subjects. It must teach moral lessons consistent with this ideal and enhance them by the emotional appeal of art.

Neither Plato nor Confucius represented an extreme attitude for his time. They were rather moderate, far-seeing intellectuals who tried to find a wise middle course. Both seem ultraconservative and repressive to the individual from the standpoint of twentieth-century liberalism. They opposed much of what we now regard as creative, democratic, and progressive. But we must consider the conditions under which they lived. Both lived in times of war, social strife, and disintegration of old orders. There was reason for them to stress unity and stability at the sacrifice of freedom and to call for the help of art in preserving civilization. There is need in histories of aesthetics for a fuller recognition of all these main conflicting approaches, Occidental and Oriental.

In the Western Renaissance, surviving Platonism discouraged a frank, full realism in the arts; lofty ideals of beauty and morality must be maintained. The same was true of Confucian influence in literature in China and

Japan. Not until recent centuries do we find there a vigorous, realistic, secular art of the novel, expressing middle-class, naturalistic attitudes and tastes but enjoyed by some in all classes. It portrayed both high and low types of character and action, with a wide range of scenes and situations comparatively true to life. The modern novel often gave free rein to the erotic imagination; it also daringly revealed corruption and hypocrisy in high places; the cruel oppression of the poor by the rich and powerful. The *Shui Hu Chuan*, a sixteenth-century Chinese novel,[122] "is a frankly revolutionary book," frowned upon by the austere Buddhists, the Confucianists, and the Ming and Manchu governments.[123] The novel grew up in China from the fourteenth century on, culminating in such masterworks as the *Chin P'ing Mei* (seventeenth) and the *Dream of the Red Chamber* (eighteenth century). As we have already noted, the orthodox aesthetic doctrines of the time ignored or belittled the novel as unworthy to be classed as art. Publication of the novels themselves was difficult and even dangerous at times; hence it was often done secretly and anonymously.[124]

In Japan of the Ukiyo-e period (especially eighteenth and nineteenth centuries), the development of realistic and erotic fiction, drawing and prints was somewhat analogous, but less opposed by persons in high places. It coincided with the rise of a wealthy middle class to power, somewhat at the expense of the old aristocracy.

The amazingly modern Lady Murasaki (eleventh cen-

[122] Translated by Pearl Buck under the title, *All Men Are Brothers*.
[123] Fitzgerald, *op. cit.*, p. 508.
[124] Robert Ruhlmann shows how the situations and characters of popular fiction reveal some Confucian indoctrination, in the attempt to make it serve official orthodoxy. But this was only partly successful. See his "Traditional Heroes in Chinese Popular Fiction," in A. F. Wright (ed.), *The Confucian Persuasion*, pp. 141–176.

tury), herself a rebel against the stilted Chinese literary canons and defying the prejudice against female intellectuals, opened the door to artistic realism in her comments on the novel. "Clearly then," she said, "it is no part of the storyteller's craft to describe only what is good or beautiful. Sometimes, of course, virtue will be his theme, and he may then make such play with it as he will. But he is just as likely to have been struck by numerous examples of vice and folly in the world around him, and about them he has exactly the same feelings; . . . they are important and must all be garnered in. Thus anything whatsoever may become the subject of a novel, provided only that it happens in this mundane life and not in some fairyland beyond our human ken." [125] There is, of course, much besides realism in *Genji*. It is also colorful, humanistic, and psychologically acute; a vivid account of the soft, delicate, aesthetically refined Heian aristocracy under strong feminine influence. Toward the end of the story its author shows more and more Buddhist piety.

Two deities, imported from India and moderately popular in early Heian times, gained a much greater following in the Kamakura. These were Kwannon (transformed from a male Bodhisattva to a female goddess of mercy) and Fudō, a ferocious and terrible male figure. The latter, it is said, became popular with the rising warrior class as a guardian of the state in times of disorder. The cult of Fudō established shrines in rocky crags and seashores where nature also is terrible. He is shown as surrounded by flames, carrying a sword and rope to strike and bind evil.[126]

[125] *The Tale of Genji*, "A Wreath of Cloud," p. 500 in the one-volume edition translated by Arthur Waley (Boston, Houghton Mifflin, n.d.).

[126] *Sources of Japanese Tradition*, p. 157.

These are a few examples of the changing social and ideological backgrounds of Oriental art, which have helped to motivate styles and subjects of representation. Except for rare instances like the terse comments of Lady Murasaki, they have not led to new theoretical principles—at least, in a form now accessible to the ordinary Western reader. The traditional cultures of India, China, and Japan were different in many important ways, but they also had much in common. The great unifying force was the flow of religious and artistic influence from India northward into China, Tibet, and Japan. What is imported, what indigenous in these northern countries is still in some dispute. It is easy to trace the progress and the gradual transformations of the images of Buddha and the Bodhisattvas in the Wei and later dynasties. Some recent historians credit India with considerable influence on Chinese painting.[127]

[127] "It is hardly possible for a western artist to appreciate the psychology and practice of oriental art without knowing that the practice of Yoga was combined with a most elaborate and scientific mnemonic system, by means of which the whole of Sanskrit literature was handed down from the Vedic period until medieval times without being committed to writing... The whole practice of the Indian, Chinese, and Japanese schools of painting was based upon methods derived from this mnemonic and psychic training, given in the universities of northern India." (E. B. Havell, *Ideals of Indian Art* [London, 1911], p. 40). Quoted by K. T. Shah, *op. cit.*, p. 111, who adds that the Indian universities of the Mauryan and Gupta eras were necessary, "not only to the professional scholar, the monk or the sannyasi, but also to all artists in the plastic, pictorial, literary, or social arts." Hiuen-Tsang, Chinese pilgrim, spent several years at these Buddhist universities and visited the Gupta court in the seventh century A.D. On the importance of the Buddhist universities and their curricula in art, see R. Mukerjee, *The Culture and Art of India*, pp. 188ff. Classical Tantric texts were translated from Sanskrit into Tibetan and from Chinese into Sanskrit. "The Indian Sahaja and the Chinese Tao are identical." (p. 288). Influence went in both directions. Havell's statement seems now to exaggerate the Indian influence on Chinese art. That influence was greater in the T'ang than in later dynasties, and its extent even then is debatable.

Among the main distinctions are: the Indian caste system, for millennia the social framework of Indian civilization; the extended clan system in China, which handled many juridical, family, and personal problems under the empire; the comparative mobility of Japanese culture through successive importations and domestic revolutions. The great diversity of the Japanese cultural inheritance, as compared with the Indian and Chinese, apparently makes it easy for the Japanese to accept further innovations, and hard for them to summarize their aesthetic philosophy in any single synthesis. Aesthetics in India and China apparently changed little during the last few centuries, although both countries developed somewhat new styles of art—e.g., Rajput painting in north India; "flung ink" brush landscape painting in the southern Sung dynasty; drama in the Yüan.

Long before the Christian era, India and China were fairly complex civilizations, at least in and around the main urban centers. Ruling dynasties had amalgamated numerous tribes and petty kingdoms into centralized military empires of increasing size. Different ethnic groups with different languages, religions, and customs were being hammered into unity against some resistance. They were on different stages of artistic and technological evolution: some still neolithic, some with flourishing bronze cultures.

Where there is conquest, followed by the domination of one group and forced labor by others, but without total elimination of the conquered, there is sure to be some discontent and potential revolt. Wherever the arts play important parts in the culture, there is a possibility of different tastes and attitudes toward them; perhaps resentment at their cost and limitation to a privileged few. Most of these feelings toward art never find lasting, written expression, but some of them do. Even when we lack all explicit docu-

mentation of them, we can often infer their nature from surviving statements condemning them, as in Plato's attacks on
popular art.

16. Changing moral and religious attitudes toward art in the ancient world

The value-system of the ruling class in early military empires is somewhat similar throughout the world. It is basi-
cally a continuation of the primitive struggle for survival,
power, and wealth under ruthless, bitterly competitive conditions. The more successful groups, having attained a temporarily secure position and an economic surplus, usually
do not and can not stop contending. They keep on fighting
and scheming for more and more power and wealth. They
must maintain an army and administrative bureaucracy to
compel or induce the people to work and fight for them.

Art plays an important part, first, in instilling the necessary habits of awe, obedience, and loyalty among the people;
secondly, in supposedly inducing the gods by worship,
prayer, and ritual to grant victory, fertility, health, and
other desiderata. Thirdly, art gives pleasure and pride to
the ruling class through magnificent display, luxurious entertainment, flattering portraits and praise of their greatness. The nature of surviving works of art from the early
empires indicates a great similarity of aims and general
functions for the arts throughout the world, but considerable diversity of the means employed—e.g., the temples,
vessels, and implements made for ritual purposes. The validity of these ends and means was so universally assumed as
to need no explicit statement or defense. But we can infer
them from the richness and amount of tangible works of art
surviving, from representations of troops of musicians and

dancers in the palace, and from proud inscriptions about the emperor's wealth and tributes, as in Egypt and Babylon. Countless repetitions of the cycle of conquests and revolts, rising and falling despotisms and briefly ruling dynasties, would make no fundamental change in the social system and its attitude toward art.

From the seventh century B.C. onwards, a number of more radical, far-reaching movements of moral and religious reform occurred in various parts of the world. Some of them grew to revolutionary proportions. They brought the question of the value of art into the open, explicitly or by implication, through denouncing the whole value-system of the military empire. That may have been done innumerable times without attracting attention, but several movements of this era won large followings and changed the course of history. Their leaders, sages and prophets from various social strata, deplored the endless round of killing and suffering which brought no lasting good to anyone. Notable among them were the Buddhists and Jains in India, the Taoists and Moists in China, the Essenes and early Christians in the Near East. To some extent (different in different times and places) they rejected the whole imperial, military enterprise, the goals of power, wealth, and sensuous pleasure on earth, the obligation of subjects to bear arms, work hard for the good of the state, obey orders, perform traditional religious rituals, and all the rest.

Neither Buddhism nor Christianity began as a directly social or political revolution; their message was moral and religious. But they had profound social and political implications and consequences: (a) in brushing aside the traditional military, imperial, and class system as irrelevant or obstructive to the good life; (b) in appealing strongly to the poor and humble, who were more attracted than others by the promise of rewards after death. The huge followings thus attracted were able to exert social and political influence, as in weakening the military ideal. The value of most kinds of art was automatically denied by sweeping injunctions against the lure of sensuous images, idolatry and vain oblations; also by denouncing the gold and banners, the sounding brass and tinkling cymbals of imperial pomp. Caste and class barriers were gently set aside by praise of poverty and humility and the examples set by Gautama and Jesus. New roads were opened to every individual, however poor, humble, and sinful, to achieve release from this bodily and social prison. On the whole the new roads were world-rejecting, if by "world" we mean the attractions of this life on earth. Some leaders promised a measure of happiness here and now through universal love, mutual service, following nature and yielding to the flow of events, but their most persuasive appeal was the promise of Heaven, Nirvana, or release from future births after death. Elaborate rituals and mortifications of the flesh, meticulous obedience to ancient laws, were all unnecessary since the path to release lay within the individual, with or without the aid of some compassionate god or saint.

What place was left for art? Practically none, in principle, as we can easily see by reading the early Buddhist sutras, the New Testament, and the Lao-Tzu.[128] The whole burden of the spiritual revolution is a denial of all the values for which imperial art had stood. There might remain some simple hymns and rhythmic prayers for the faithful; noth-

---

[128] "[The disciple] keeps aloof from dance, song, music, and the visiting of shows; rejects flowers, perfumes, ointment, as well as every kind of adornment and embellishment. High and gorgeous beds he does not use. . . . Women and girls he does not accept. He owns no male and female slaves, owns no goats, sheep, fowls, pigs, elephants, cows or horses, no land and goods." From the Pāli scripture *Anguttara-Nikaya* in *A Buddhist Bible* (Thetford, Vt., Goddard, 1938). The Pāli books are fairly close to early, Hinayana Buddhism.

ing visual or tangible; no complex music or literature. Any attachment to external, sensory stimuli was an obstacle to release, and that included practically the whole world of art. If not denounced explicitly, art was excluded in principle as involving sensual delights, costly expenditure, pride of power and wealth, oppression of the poor, and sometimes idolatry. Art is hardly mentioned in the *New Testament*.[129] At this stage in the ascetic movement there is little or no artistic expression. All luxury, display, and sensuous pleasure have been renounced. Simple verbal and musical expressions such as sermons, letters, hymns and prayers may remain; also simple drawings as in the Catacombs. Costly architecture, fine furniture and clothing, elaborate entertainments, are all shunned as parts of the hated old régime. Countless millions took the new roads out of political life and away from all its artistic attractions. Some leaders and followers went to fanatical extremes; some compromised a little with the requirements of organized society.

If all humanity had acted fully in accord with the most extreme of world-rejecting leaders, there would be no society and no humanity on earth today. Their advice was biologically fatal: a certain course to race suicide through asceticism and celibacy. No society can endure on earth without someone to get and distribute food and shelter and someone to protect the group from predatory enemies. Governments and laws of some sort must be set up and people must obey them on the whole. Enough individuals must reproduce and raise children to assure survival of the species. Moreover, mere survival is not enough to satisfy a people which has tasted the joys of civilization. It is a bleak

[129] One of the few references is that in Matthew 24, where Jesus says of the temple, "See ye not all these things? Verily I say unto you, There shall not be left here one stone upon another, that shall not be thrown down." Another is Paul's denunciation of the silversmiths of Ephesus for making figurines of Diana.

world without art. One can hope to secure and enjoy a modest amount of this world's goods by doing the kind of work for which one is fitted, without going to the opposite extreme of violent rapacity. Hence compromises were made; most people stayed within the social system. A place was made for those inclined to the priestly, the monastic or the hermit life. Others went on working, fighting, begetting, raising families as best they could. Art also survived.

Gradually, at different times in different regions, the social system itself improved a little, became less cruel and combative, at least under benevolent kings. A more moderate kind of moral reformer arose here and there: notably Confucius in the East; Socrates and Plato in the West. They rejected the old imperial policy of unlimited conquest, seizure, and luxury through exploitation. But they did approve of centralized government, military defense, work according to one's abilities, raising children, performing rituals in honor of the gods and the state, and producing some kinds of art.

Here we enter the realm of extant, philosophic aesthetics, for Plato, Confucius, and their followers have told us what kinds of art are to be cultivated in the ideal state. It is to be a just though somewhat regimented state, as necessary in troublous times; a state in which each individual does what he is best fitted for. Individuals, families and classes are to live in harmony with each other under wise, civilized laws and rulers. The kind of art to be permitted is that which reinforces this ideal system aesthetically and emotionally. It will raise the soul from bestial materialism to awareness of universal principles as applied to human conduct, but not necessarily to complete abandonment of the sensuous, natural world. Some followers of Plato and Confucius, as always, carried their teachings to extremes in various directions.

In India, one persistent source of disagreement was the Aryan conquest and the subsequent partial merging of the conquerors with the Dravidian and other aborigines. We have referred above to Zimmer's controversial theory that the two psychological strains, the two opposing world-views, persist throughout Indian art and aesthetics to the present time: the Vedic Aryan being predominantly vigorous, military, dominating, sensuous, and world-accepting; the Dravidian being yogic, mystical, and world-rejecting. Whether or not such a clear-cut opposition existed along racial lines, it appears that the two world-views were partly merged on a rational level soon after the Vedic period, in the Brahmanas and Upanishads; also in the arts. Anyone could choose to emphasize either in his life, although one's occupation and responsibilities were somewhat prescribed according to birth. In theories of art, as we have seen, the two were combined in Kama and Moksha as approved aims of life and in the conception of aesthetic experience as occurring on various levels, the mystic at the top. In Hinduism, the conceptions of the gods and their iconographies in visual art and story were not committed to extreme asceticism. Many deities, such as Vishnu, were robustly physical and sexual in their incarnations. The two great epics glorified both military heroism and spiritual holiness. Universal mystic symbolism helped the mind to interrelate sensuous appearance and illusion, as in the drama, with metaphysical meanings. Thus Indian civilization was expanded and enriched by the incorporation and partial reconciliation of different attitudes toward life and art, including (a) the ancient, military, imperial system, (b) the radically ascetic, renunciative system, and (c) more moderate, rational ideals directed toward social justice and diversity of values for the individual life, including the aesthetic.

Significant changes occurred also in the great moral-religious movements, as traditions descending through the ages. Both Buddhism and Christianity went through a typical series of transformations, especially with respect to their attitudes toward art. (Somewhat analogous changes have occurred in other great, long-lived religions.) The first stage, as we have just observed, was that of ascetic renunciation of the world, including all but the simplest, plainest vestiges of art. The second stage is that of rise to power, wealth, and luxury. This occurred, for example, in the accession of Asoka as the first Buddhist Emperor in India (c. 270 B.C.) and in that of Constantine as first Christian Emperor of Rome (c. 306 A.D.).

This rise tends to liberate and stimulate an era of great magnificence, with a radically altered attitude toward art, especially in the service of Church and Empire. The ascetic and anti-artistic principles of the founders are set aside and perhaps replaced by personal worship of the founder and his associates. Hostility and destructiveness toward certain aspects of the previous religion and its art are likely. Reaction against those formerly in power and the old established system may motivate new styles of art, such as Indian Buddhist painting and Byzantine mosaic. Some writers, such as St. Augustine (in the *Confessions*) have difficulty in reconciling the beauties of art with the ascetic teachings of the founder. This may raise the moral problem of whether art is always bad because sensual, or good when used for the glory of God and the Church. That problem worried medieval aestheticians throughout the Middle Ages. Monastic orders were provided for those who wished an ascetic life. Buddhism died out in India by the ninth century, but rose to power in China (Wei dynasty) and Japan with renewed bursts of artistic expression and magnificent display.

In the third stage the new religion is accepted and incorporated in the established system, not necessarily in control, but as one respected tradition among others. It becomes more tolerant and compromising. Buddhism sank to this status in China when Confucianism revived. It altered its views considerably, becoming more positive, nature-loving, and artistic, while still favoring simplicity and kindness in accord with its early teachings. In India, much of early Buddhism was incorporated in Hinduism, including respect for gentler, meditative methods of seeking enlightenment as opposed to the extreme asceticism and ritualism of ancient Brahmanism. This included more respect for the arts as possible means of attaining enlightenment.

In China both Buddhism and Taoism changed, merged partly, and influenced the arts. They stood at times for the free, relaxed, informal, broadly humanistic type of art; at times for unrestrained polytheism, also represented in art. Later Buddhist and later Christian philosophers have become more tolerant of other creeds and ways of life. They have become less ascetic while usually discouraging extreme, costly display except in the service of religion or the state. A single work of art in China may combine Confucian, Taoist, and Buddhist traits. Likewise in the European Renaissance, Christian art incorporated pagan traits. The early Christian antagonism toward pagan religion and art decreased, and both were respected as parts of Western civilization.

This third stage in the reformist movement is usually characterized by mildness, partial acceptance of other views, lack of strong partisanship, and catholicity of taste in art. The new religion has succeeded in reforming the old system somewhat, though not as much as had been hoped, and has become more liberal in the process. Note, for instance, the acceptance by St. Thomas of Aristotelian ideas and Dante's admiration for Virgil and the Roman imperial ideal.

In contrast with the Hinayana Buddhist tendency to prohibit or depreciate art, as shown in the Pāli scriptures, later (Mahayana) Buddhism encouraged it. This it did, not only by providing a new pantheon of Bodhisattvas, gods, and demons to represent, but also by encouraging the construction and decoration of stupas, shrines, and temples. A valuable article by Professor A. C. Soper summarizes his search for references to painting in Chinese translations of Buddhist literature.[130] They cover the whole of Buddhist writings, he says, including the time and place when sculpture and painting "were first being granted high importance as a religious instrument: i.e., North India in the first two or three centuries of the Christian era." This was "before the final organization of art under Tantric stimulus, roughly from the eighth century on." The dates of the original scriptures cannot be exactly determined. A single text may contain accumulated, somewhat inconsistent material from many generations.

Professor Soper's quotations, arranged so far as possible in the order given by their sources, represent "every shade of opinion, from a prohibition as final as the Semitic to the fullest iconolatry." They begin with a supposed order to nuns by the Buddha, not to look at paintings in a pagan temple. When people in a later stage wish to practice art, it is, of course, easy enough to interpolate a passage wherein the Founder is made to approve it. Later quotations show the Buddha explicitly directing how a stupa is to be constructed and painted; with what colors, figures, etc. In some, restrictions are imposed (as against portraying the Buddha himself, or any living creatures); in others, the "chain of events in the Buddha's career" is to be shown in great detail in many colors. They proved, it is said, "an effective aid in

[130] "Early Buddhist Attitudes toward the Art of Painting," *Art Bulletin*, XXXII, 2 (June 1950), pp. 147–151.

spiritual advancement." On one occasion "Pusya Buddha mixed various pigments and with His own hand made a painting of one image to serve as a model. From that the masters did 84,000 images to be bestowed upon the various lands, so that the monarchs there might be able to worship them." In a previous age, according to one story, a crown prince knew the arts and was an excellent painter. For painting a picture of Buddha in a former life he was now rewarded by being born in a royal house.

Buddhism began to flourish in Japan under the regency of Prince Shotoku (592–622). Many ornate temples were built thereafter, especially in and near the capital at Nara. Monasteries were embellished with sculptures, mural and hanging paintings, and tapestries. Scrolls of texts and narratives were produced in great numbers. "The history of Buddhism and Buddhist art in Japan," says Philip S. Rawson, "was closely bound up with the support received from courts and powerful individuals or families. . . The great size and splended adornment of Japan's Buddhist monasteries was a direct reflection of the interest of the ruling caste of the country." Important religious functions were assigned to art, as in serving to focus the mind vividly upon the images and their symbolic meanings.[131] Several varieties of Buddhism arose in Japan; one (called Mantra or Shingon Buddhism) derived from Tantric India by way of China. In this, magical powers were attributed to painting through the use of ancient Sanskrit spells.

The history of a great, long-lived religion is, of course, not limited to the three stages roughly distinguished above. Many religions are flexible enough to allow different, even contrary movements at the same time. Some try to revive

[131] *Japanese Paintings from Buddhist Shrines and Temples.* Introduction by Philip S. Rawson (New York, Mentor-Unesco Art Books, 1963), pp. 5–15.

the primitive type while others press on to more highly evolved syntheses with elements of science or other religions. In all of these movements, attitudes toward art are likely to change accordingly. The foregoing section does not imply a theory of definite, universal stages. The diversities of cultural history are enormous. From the fact of a certain sequence in India, one cannot expect to find it also in Japan. Analogies exist, but their extent is still problematic.

17. What are "spiritual values"?
Metaphysical assumptions
of Oriental aesthetics

The religious and metaphysical basis of most Oriental theories of art constitutes a serious obstacle to their acceptance by Western scholars. This is not a set of vague theological beliefs, somewhere in the remote background; it permeates the texture of almost all theoretical discussions of art, especially in India. It is "supernaturalistic" in a sense opposed to "naturalistic." The latter term characterizes Western science and the philosophy based upon it, as well as the approach of many Western scholars and historians to art and aesthetics. There are endless varieties of supernaturalism and approximate synonyms for that word, such as transcendentalism, spiritualism, pantheism, panpsychism, idealism (in the metaphysical sense), dualism, and mysticism. Many volumes have been written on the subtle distinctions among philosophic schools in India, such as the monumental series by S. Dasgupta.[132] Some Indian sects are described as "atheistic," "materialistic," "naturalistic," and the like, but this is true only in a very limited, relative sense;

[132] *A History of Indian Philosophy.*

only the ancient, long-dead Carvaka school deserved those epithets. Buddhism has been called "atheistic," but this is far from the truth as applied to Mahayana Buddhism. Hinduism in India, Buddhism and Taoism in China and Japan, Shinto in Japan, are all essentially supernaturalistic in asserting the independence of spirit from matter and physical bodies. Some varieties of supernaturalism are also widely believed in the West, such as Platonic and Hegelian idealism and Thomistic dualism. Adherents of these creeds may feel a certain general kinship with Oriental supernaturalism, but most of them refuse to accept the specific theology, eschatology, cosmology, and ethics of Oriental religions. In general, Christians, Jews, and Moslems are not enthusiastic about the idea of union with a world spirit conceived along Hindu lines. Western naturalists reject both Eastern and Western varieties of idealism and other supernaturalist creeds.

In view of this wide gulf between the Eastern and Western world-views, the question arises in aesthetics as it has in many East-West conferences on philosophy and religion, of whether any common ground of agreement can be found between them. That question can be largely focused on the single concept of "spiritual values," a term which recurs very often in Oriental writing on art and aesthetics as well as in other branches of philosophy.[133]

[133] For an Indian opinion on the concept as seen from both points of view, see "The Concept of the Spiritual in Eastern and Western Thought," in *Comparative Studies in Philosophy in Honor of Radhakrishnan* (New York, Harper, n.d.), pp. 189ff. The conference report edited by Charles A. Moore, *Essays in East-West Philosophy* (Honolulu, Univ. of Hawaii, 1951), contains almost nothing on art or aesthetics. It does contain a good deal of rather vague dogmatizing on "spirituality" and "spiritual values." The Oriental (especially Indian) philosophers seem much more sure of what they believe than the Occidental ones do. The Occidental philosophers disagree among

PLATE VIII. *Indian Yantra: the Sri Cakra,*
or Wheel of Fortune. One of many types of geometrical
figures symbolizing gods, men, and animals.
Its inner meaning, to be grasped through yoga, is
the nature of the deity. (Courtesy of P. J. Chaudhury).

PLATE IX.
Sesshu,
Haboku (flung ink)
Landscape.
Hanging scroll.
(The Cleveland Museum
of Art, Gift of the
Norweb Foundation).

It is taken for granted in most of the leading world religions, East and West, that there is a realm of spiritual existence, independent of matter; a transcendental level of reality superior to that of nature and ordinary human experience, on which divine and other incorporeal spirits live and think. "Spirit" is an entity, a real and eternal substance, according to this view.[134] Many would go as far as to call this belief essential to any kind of religion, although there have been materialistic forms of theism.[135] Some of the manifestations of spirit, as in individual gods like Krishna, may be conceived as aspects of a Supreme Deity or ideas in a Cosmic Mind.

We have noted the widely held belief that man can rise into the spiritual realm through proper self-discipline, there to enjoy the blissful contemplation of, or union with, the

themselves, but some of them lean over backwards in acknowledging the faults of Western civilization and the "spiritual greatness" of the East. The Oriental contributions tend to be mere elementary summaries of traditional beliefs. They make practically no concession to Western science or naturalistic philosophy, in spite of the often-stated hope for a "world synthesis" in philosophy. Sri Aurobindo, "On Philosophical Synthesis," is an example of boundless assurance as to the spiritual pre-eminence of Indian thought. *Philosophy East and West*, Jan. 1963, quoting his *The Riddle of This World* (Calcutta, Arya, 1946). For some discerning comments on Indian assumptions of spiritual superiority, see Joseph Campbell's "The Cultural Setting of Asian Art," cited above.

[134] Webster's *Third New International Dictionary* (1961) provides the following definitions consistent with this belief: "spirit:... 2b: a supernatural, incorporeal, rational being or personality, usually invisible to human beings but having the power to become so at will... d: a being having an incorporeal or immaterial nature ('God is a spirit'). 4b: a disembodied soul existing as an independent entity; the soul departed from the body of a deceased person... 9. Life or consciousness having an independent type of existence. 'Idealists maintain that the essential nature of the universe is spirit.' "

[135] The Epicureans disbelieved in spirit, but held that the gods are composed of atoms as humans are. A religion can be atheistic, as in Auguste Comte's "religion of humanity."

119

divine Being. Aesthetics enters the religious picture in that art (the right kind of art) is sometimes held to be a means of elevating the human mind toward that higher realm, by freeing it from the bonds of earthly attachment and helping it to regard this life in a more universal, impersonal way. The value of art can then be judged on the basis of how well it helps in this liberating, spiritualizing process.

In most forms of supernaturalism, there is also a belief in the mystic experience as a source of true knowledge of the spiritual realm: that is, a belief in sources other than the senses, including dreams, trances, and revelations. The mystic experience is also regarded as one of the highest, most blissful types of experience in its own right.

The lasting kinship between Oriental, medieval European, and modern European mysticism is manifested in an emphasis on the so-called "spiritual values" of art; the term "spiritual" being conceived in terms of a supernaturalist theology. Supernaturalists of all religious creeds tend to emphasize the mystical attitude toward art and aesthetic experience and the role of "spiritual power" in causing it. As we have seen, many concepts used in Oriental aesthetics, such as *rasa, satori, yūgen,* and "spirit resonance," tend to suggest a supernatural cause and explanation, either in the artist, the work of art, the observer, or all of these.

Coomaraswamy gives an explicitly spiritualistic interpretation to some of them in his essay, "The Theory of Art in Asia." [136] The First Canon of Hsieh Ho on "operation of the spirit in life movement" is, he says, "of primary metaphysical importance." Ch'an Zen art seeks "realization of the divine being in man" by "opening his eyes to a like spiritual essence in the world of Nature." Pure aesthetic experience, or the tasting of *rasa,* says Coomaraswamy (paraphrasing the Sahitya Darpana) "is theirs in whom the knowledge

[136] *The Transformation of Nature in Art,* pp. 3, 19–20, 40, 47, 54.

of ideal beauty is innate; it is known intuitively, in intellectual ecstasy . . . born of one mother with the vision of God, its life is as it were a flash of blinding light of transmundane origin." Both *rasa* and *dhvani* (overtone of meaning) are essentially metaphysical and Vedantic, he adds, and Indian aesthetics is "universal," identical in essentials with the Far Eastern and Scholastic Christian views and that of William Blake.

18. The naturalistic conception of spiritual values

Philosophic naturalists doubt or deny the existence of "spirit" as an entity or substance, especially in the form of incorporeal spirits having power to live, think, and act independently of material bodies. They doubt or deny the existence of incorporeal gods, angels, devils, demons, fairies, ghosts or disembodied souls of the dead, and the like. They do *not* deny the existence of "spiritual activities" or "spiritual experience" if it is defined in a naturalistic way. "Spiritual" in this sense refers to the more highly developed aesthetic, intellectual, and moral types of thought and experience: those which are broadly philosophical, humanitarian, or universal in range and interest as opposed to the narrowly selfish satisfaction of bodily appetites and activities devoted thereto. But all of these, the naturalist holds, are the activities of brains and nervous systems in highly evolved, living bodies; they cannot operate independently and they involve no distinct, incorporeal substance.[137] Ac-

---

[137] Use of the word "spiritual" in this context is recognized in Webster's *Third New International Dictionary* (1961) as follows: "spiritual: . . . 7. of, relating to, or coming from the intellectual and higher endowments of the mind." The term "mind" is also defined accordingly: not as an independent entity, but as the functioning of certain parts of the bodily mechanism, especially the cortical.

cording to this view, there is no mysterious "spiritual power" (*yūgen*) apart from a physical basis.

Naturalists hold that thought, feeling, imagination, desire, joy, pleasure, bliss, ecstasy, the creation and appreciation of art, are all quite real *as phenomena*, but consist in the activities of complex brains and nervous systems in highly evolved living organisms such as man. The naturalist can speak of "mind," "mental," "psychic" and "spiritual" phenomena, activities, experiences, etc.; but he understands them all as activities of the brain and nervous system. Likewise the idealist can speak without inconsistency of "body," "matter," "physical," and "corporeal" phenomena, while conceiving them as ideas in a divine, cosmic mind.

Many such philosophic terms are metaphysically neutral in isolation. They refer to phenomena which can be variously explained. They are capable of being used in different, contradictory philosophic systems when redefined accordingly. Thus "transcendental" to an idealist means "extending above the world of the senses and of matter; rising above the contingent particularity of ordinary experience." If used by a naturalist or empiricist to designate something real and actual, he must define it in a more limited way. One cannot rise entirely above and out of the world of sensory experience, he will say, but one can rise to a psychologically and ethically higher level within it. One can rise above the petty, self-conscious preoccupations of ordinary life with its sordid penny-pinching, its trivial squabbles and meannesses, to see life steadily and see it whole, *sub specie aeternitatis*. A naturalist can agree with the mystic that something of the sort takes place in the response of suitably trained and educated observers to great art. He will insist, however, that there is nothing supernatural about it.

Naturalists do not deny the reality or importance of what they regard as "spiritual values"—that is, of the values achieved in highly developed mental and moral experience in art and other fields. They do not minimize the value of such experience in civilized human life. They agree that religious activities on earth provide many important spiritual values, which are not necessarily dependent on the truth of the creed concerned. All the great Eastern and Western religions have provided such values. But it is a mistake, according to naturalism, to regard these values as supernaturally caused, or to restrict the concept of "spiritual value" to those concerned with theistic religion. Spiritual values, in a broad sense, can be produced and achieved in many fields of secular activity, such as philosophy, art, and science, especially as these are used to benefit humanity.

It is a misconception, unfortunately common in the Orient, to suppose that Occidentals reject or disparage spiritual values in this ethical sense, and devote themselves mainly to food and drink, dollars, machinery, and atomic bombs. Moral, aesthetic, and intellectual activities are not necessarily lowered in value through being explained as products of natural evolution and as motions of complex bodily mechanisms. Naturalistic and humanistic philosophers regard the creation of great art, the relief of poverty and disease on earth, the establishment of social justice, as spiritual values achievable through Western methods. The kind of value which Oriental supernaturalists rate most highly, that of "breaking the cycle of rebirths" or "union with the Absolute Self" is regarded by naturalists as non-existent and impossible; as purely imaginary and hence worthless, except for any incidental values achieved in pursuing it during one's life on earth.

This is a clear-cut issue between contradictory beliefs. It cannot be settled while both parties to it cling to their fundamental positions. If the spiritualists are right, the naturalists are blind to the essential nature of the world and man and to the highest values of life. If the naturalists are right, the spiritualists are credulous, wishful thinkers, clinging to ancient myths and superstitions for which there is not a shred of scientific or empirical evidence. They are perpetuating primitive modes of thought long since abandoned by science in both hemispheres. Neither side can prove its case.

In the West, philosophic naturalism under one name or another has been a major tradition since Democritus, Epicurus, and Lucretius. Aristotle was in some respects a naturalist, especially as to art. After centuries of dormancy in Christian Rome and the Middle Ages, naturalism revived in Europe in the seventeenth and eighteenth centuries. Incomplete and groping in the theories of Hobbes, Gassendi, La Mettrie, and some of the Encyclopedists, it has received increasing support from science up to the present time; especially from Darwinian evolution and physiological psychology. It received support from the empiricism of Francis Bacon, Locke, and Hume, even though these men were not complete naturalists. It achieved some fullness of statement in Spencer, Dewey, Russell, and Santayana.

The basic tenets of naturalism have been obscured by a multiplicity of names for individual variants, referring to different aspects of the naturalistic world-view. It has been called "atomism" or "materialism" with respect to its ontology and cosmology, "empiricism" or "positivism" with respect to its epistemology, "hedonism" and "eudaemonism" with respect to its ethics, "mechanism" with respect to its biology.

The term "naturalism" is highly ambiguous today. Some European writers associate it with the literary movement typified by Émile Zola; some confuse it with existentialism and some with Marxism, which is only one variety of the naturalistic world-view. Even in Europe, many students do not realize that there is any kind of naturalistic philosophy except the Marxist. In art, the term "naturalism" is often applied to the painting and sculpture of the Renaissance, in the sense of accurate representation of the visual appearance of things in the natural world. Such ambiguity is hard to avoid in an age of rapid cultural change. It exists with regard to other philosophic concepts, such as idealism.

One kind of naturalism is developed into a thoroughgoing system of philosophy, with explicit theories on all the main perennial problems. Another kind is only an attitude of mind, a strong interest in and respect for things of this world. In this latter sense, a considerable number of Western scholars in the arts and humanities are naturalistic, whatever religious or philosophic creed they profess. They may be metaphysical dualists or spiritualists, but their interests are more in things of this life than in fantasies of heaven or hell. Their methods of thought are empirical and rational, not mystical. They interpret mystic symbolism in art as a cultural phenomenon which can be described and explained without introducing supernatural factors.

Some philosophers continue to use the traditional term "spirit" while defining it in a naturalistic way. "Spirit," says George Santayana, "is an awareness natural to animals, revealing the world and themselves in it. Spirit is only that inner light of . . . attention which floods all life . . . It is roughly the same as feeling or thought." [138] Such writers do not confuse metaphysical idealism with "having high ideals" or metaphysical materialism with "devotion to material goods."

In the naturalistic sense of "spirit" and "spiritual," it can be said that all art is spiritual. All art involves some perceptual and imaginative reorganization in terms of a sensory medium of form and expression. It is a communica-

[138] *The Realm of Spirit* in *Realms of Being* (New York, Scribner's, 1942), pp. 549ff.

tion of one perceiving, thinking, feeling animal to others. But all art is not equally spiritual. Some remains closer to the physical basis of life: e.g., in appealing to primary somatic or sexual appetites, as in a realistic advertising poster of food or in an erotic photograph of a nude figure. Some art has little creative originality, little departure from everyday, mundane concerns, little transformation of the products of nature and past art. Some art is more spiritual in that it deals more creatively with mental, imaginative, aesthetic, moral, or intellectual experience.

But it is not to be assumed that the more spiritual art is always better. That must be decided on other grounds. Art may be very spiritual and of little value at times, or vice versa.

Van Meter Ames, in an essay on "Aesthetic Values in the East and West," [139] agrees with John Dewey that "all normal human interest can attain a spiritual level through artistic expression. The spiritual value of art then inheres in clarifying and intensifying values which are already there." Ames is not much concerned about the ambiguity of "spiritual" or its strongly mystical associations in Oriental aesthetics. Many Western philosophers, however, try to avoid the term. Frequent reference to "spiritual values" by visiting Indian swamis and devotees of Zen repels the more tough-minded Western scholars. To them, it has come to sound objectionably sanctimonious and supercilious. Too often in recent years, the Oriental scholars who emphasize this term also imply that the East has almost a monopoly on spiritual values; that all the West's endeavors are on a lower plane. This does not make intellectual cooperation any easier. An American critic has recently declared that " 'Spiritual' is today so full of connotations of

[139] *Journal of Aesthetics and Art Criticism*, XIX, 1 (Fall 1960), pp. 3ff.

cultism, occultism, and trailing chiffon that even organized religions shun the word." [140]

19. The naturalistic attitude toward mystic experience

While denying the divine inspiration of the artist and the supernatural status of his power, naturalism is quite ready to accept the *phenomenal* reality of the various kinds of mystic, ecstatic, and intuitive experience which are cultivated so assiduously in the Orient. No doubt some people actually do have these strange ecstasies and visions, these feelings of being united with a higher power. Zen and yoga are undoubtedly effective as techniques along this line. Certain drugs are said to cause similar experiences. Obviously, many Oriental adepts have developed powers of bodily, mental, and emotional self-control far beyond anything commonly attempted in the West. Man's marvelous bodily mechanism, which we in the West educate to do certain things well, can doubtless be trained to do very different things, which we can hardly imagine.

It may well be that the resulting kinds of experience have not only great intrinsic value for their own sake as blissful ecstasy, but also instrumental value as aids to creative inspiration for the artist. This is quite consistent with the naturalistic belief that they are somehow physiological in basis and will be ultimately open to investigation by empirical science. In the history of art, one must recognize the fact that Ch'an in China, Zen in Japan, and Christian mysticism in medieval Europe, have all been potent stimuli to art. Some of the art thus produced has been great, but not all;

[140] F. Bultman, "The Achievement of Hans Hofmann," in *Art News*, Sept. 1963, p. 54.

much stereotyped and mediocre art is also produced by followers of these methods. When a great artist like Seami is a follower of Zen, to what extent is his greatness due to that method, and to what extent to other cultural factors or to innate ability? Assuming that it works well in a congenial Oriental setting, to what extent can it be exported or practiced successfully in the rationalistic atmosphere of the West? Such questions are sure to be asked more and more by tough-minded scholars. They bear upon the question, asked at the start of this book, of what value Oriental aesthetics can have for the West.

These questions are answered favorably by Van Meter Ames in the essay just cited. He praises the positive contributions of Zen to art in the West as well as the East. He minimizes its supernaturalist element and emphasizes the "stress on creativity," the "fresh and vivid dynamism," the "sense of depth, of power in reserve, and vital freedom." [141] He likens Zen to John Dewey's aesthetics (*Art as Experience*) in that the latter stresses "the continuity of art and life, regarding art as the clarification and completion of what experience normally is or tends to be." Both oppose, he says, the formalistic separation of art from daily life. Other American philosophers would emphasize Dewey's praise for intelligent planning and logical analysis, as opposed to the irrationalism and intuitionism of Zen. Arthur Koestler takes a strongly negative, derogatory attitude toward Zen in modern Japan, while granting it some values as an antidote to excessive formalism.[142] Toward yoga he is even more antagonistic. Both Zen and pragmatism, Eastern and Western aesthetics, are many-sided. Each contains

[141] *Op. cit.,* pp. 8, 11. Alan W. Watts is even more laudatory in *The Spirit of Zen* (London, Murray, 1936), esp. pp. 67ff on the experience of *satori.*

[142] *The Lotus and the Robot* (New York, 1961).

diverse and sometimes contrary attitudes. Much depends on which interpreters of each theory one reads.

The obvious kinship which I have analyzed in a previous section, between Oriental and medieval European mysticism, can be explained in two ways. One, which is favored by the supernaturalists, is to regard the long and wide acceptance of this world-view as evidence of its universal truth. Coomaraswamy and Aldous Huxley describe it as *philosophia perennis*. This explanation implies that Western empirical science and naturalism are merely modern errors, aberrations from the truth.

The other, from the standpoint of naturalism and cultural evolution, is to regard the Oriental world-view as an example of cultural lag or retarded intellectual development. From this point of view it seems that Oriental culture has remained up to recent years in a stage of social and intellectual evolution similar to that which Europe reached in the Middle Ages. That state was characterized by the persistence of feudal and aristocratic institutions, hereditary distinctions, traditionalism in thought, mystic symbolism, primitive technology, and the lack of organized scientific inquiry. Heinrich Zimmer remarks that Indian philosophy always lacked the "fructifying contact with progressive natural science." [143] Philosophy in India, one may add, has always remained in the service of religious tradition and artistic imagination, never submitting its assertions to the rigorous test of empirical evidence and logical reasoning. Europe made a start toward outgrowing this state in ancient Greece, and after a long setback resumed its advance toward modernity in the late Renaissance. The Far East is now struggling to catch up rapidly in material technology, in spite of its traditional scorn for such efforts. The West is also in the throes of trying to eliminate many obsolete survivals from

[143] *Philosophies of India* (New York, Pantheon, 1951), pp. 30ff.

the past. What is popularly regarded as a failure of science there can also be interpreted as a lack of sufficient reliance on scientific thinking in the field of human conduct.

To describe Oriental thought as in some ways more primitive than Occidental does not imply that it is necessarily wrong or inferior in these ways. Evolution from one cultural stage to another often entails a loss of values and of true insights. For that reason it is well to continue scrutinizing traditional beliefs, attitudes, and methods, such as those of Oriental and medieval aesthetics, to see what elements of value in them should be revived and preserved. As we keep rereading Plato and Aristotle for ideas of permanent value, we should add such Eastern names as Bharata, Abhinavagupta, Lu Chi, Liu Hsieh, and Seami to the list.

20. Inadequate knowledge of Western philosophy on the part of Oriental writers. Lack of naturalistic philosophy in the Far East

One consequence of the basic sympathy between Eastern and Western supernaturalists appears in their writings on comparative aesthetics. When the Eastern philosopher undertakes to summarize Western aesthetics, he tends to include only writers of the idealistic or dualistic persuasion. He ignores those of other schools of thought or dismisses them briefly as hardly worthy of attention. He accepts common, inaccurate clichés of thought, such as the confusion of metaphysical materialism with a materialistic attitude toward values. Highly unfair and inadequate accounts of Western philosophy in general are given in several recent comparative studies of Eastern and Western thought—notably the *History of Philosophy Eastern and Western*, edited by S. Radhakrishnan and others.[144]

The basic idea of a naturalistic philosophy or theory of art seems strange and incomprehensible to many Oriental philosophers, especially in India. This is not surprising in view of the fact that there has never been a fully developed, naturalistic system of philosophy in the Far East. The nearest thing to it in India was the ancient Carvaka school, mentioned above as corresponding roughly to Epicureanism in Greece. Supposedly founded by Brhaspati Laukya of the Rig-Veda, it attracted a following as a skeptical revolt from the prevailing spiritualism, but the latter soon overwhelmed it. The Carvakas proposed an ontological materialism, empiricism, rationalism, and hedonism. They denounced superstitious fear of the gods and of a future life. Like Epicureanism, this school of philosophy has been persistently distorted and misrepresented by the supernaturalists. None of its original texts have survived. Most Indian histories of philosophy treat it briefly and scornfully, as a crude and fleshly type of naïve hedonism. In the last few years, it has drawn more attention from scholars as modern naturalism rises in influence throughout the world.[145]

[144] (London, 1953). Volume II, Parts III and IV are devoted to Western philosophy as seen by Eastern thinkers. There is no chapter on naturalism, but it is mentioned briefly twice. The chapter on "Pragmatism" (B. Ray) is fairly good; the one on "Evolutionism" (P. S. Naidu) is a perfunctory caricature of the philosophy of Herbert Spencer. Under "Existentialism," R. V. Das gives a definition of naturalism which is again a mere caricature. With naturalism, he asserts, "there goes a steady deterioration in the quality of life lived, resulting in inner vacuity, boredom and restlessness of spirit." (p. 423). Once again it is hinted that everything true and wise in Western philosophy is Indian in origin.

[145] See the brief but comparatively fair and objective treatment by D. Bhattacharya, "The Carvaka Philosophy," in *History of Philosophy East and West*, Ch. VII. Also D. Riepe, *The Naturalistic Tradition in Indian Thought* (Seattle, Wash., 1961). Here some naturalistic ele-

If more is discovered about the Carvaka teachings, it will be interesting to see whether they contain any reference to the arts. The same question remains in regard to the teachings of Epicurus. There is little reference to them in the surviving fragments of his own writing, but much in that of his followers, notably Lucretius and Horace.

In China, Confucianism and Taoism are sometimes called naturalistic, but this is true only in a limited sense of the word. They did not evolve any system of naturalistic philosophy. Early Confucianism was somewhat naturalistic or humanistic in being interested mainly in things of this world; in the best way of life for human beings here and now.[146] Later Confucianism, in its *Li-ch'i* dualism, evolved a partial analogue to the Western dualism of spirit and matter. Neither Confucianism nor any other important Chinese or Japanese tradition seriously disputed the existence of spirits, as in gods, demons, and the souls of departed ancestors. Early Taoism was naturalistic in the sense of trying to follow nature, but the "nature" it imagined in later centuries was full of gods and spirits, good and bad. Its thinking was anti-rationalistic and favorable to magic and mysticism.

Under Buddhist and Taoist influence the ancient, animistic or hylozoic conception of nature as animated by a life force, a spirit of heaven and earth, found artistic expression in the nature-poetry and landscape painting of China and Japan. Thoughts of rebirth and of gods, devils, heavens and

---

ments in later Indian systems, especially the Samkhya, are traced. *Cf.* S. Radhakrishnan and C. A. Moore, *A Source Book in Indian Philosophy* (Princeton, 1957), pp. 227ff; also S. Dasgupta, *History of Indian Philosophy*, III, pp. 512ff.

[146] Wing-tsit Chan describes Hsün Tzu as representing the naturalistic tendency of ancient Confucianism; Mencius the idealistic. Wang Ch'ung in the first century A.D. was naturalistic in rejecting teleology. (*Source Book in Chinese Philosophy*, pp. 115, 292, 299).

hells were often pushed somewhat backward, out of the main areas of artistic representation. India, China, and Japan all produced art which is obviously religious and art which is apparently secular—naturalistic in the broad, non-philosophical sense—in spite of the absence of naturalistic philosophy. As we have seen, however, all art can be given a mystic, symbolic interpretation if one desires to do so.

21. Selecting acceptable elements in Oriental aesthetics

In rejecting the supernaturalism which pervades much Oriental aesthetics, must the Western naturalist reject its theories entirely? I think not. It is always possible to separate ideas which come to us in clusters; which first arose as parts of closely interwoven systems. One can detach them for separate consideration and perhaps combine them with others from one's own world-view.

In general, I have tried to show that the elements in Oriental aesthetics which have most value in the West are not the mystic, transcendental ones which Oriental philosophers themselves tend to emphasize. They are the records of direct experience on this earth with art, artists, and observers of art, the psychological and social insights of great artists and critics, which are organized in such theories as that of *rasa*. Much of this knowledge and grasp of values has been derived from practical, everyday artistic and aesthetic activity which is not too far from that of Western experience to permit mutual understanding. A great Western stage director, such as Stanislavsky, would have much to say to Seami and Abhinavagupta, and they to him. The naturalistic, humanistic values which abound in Indian, Chinese, and Japanese art are relatively universal. Thinkers on both sides can profit from comparing their own experience, their conceptions of what art is and ought to be, with that of others. In this way it may be possible to avoid religious and metaphysical controversy except when this is expressly desired.

I do not propose that we conceal the religious and metaphysical elements in our aesthetic theories, but that we try to distinguish them from the more empirical elements which are more widely acceptable. Also, I propose that we state our religious and metaphysical assumptions *as beliefs;* not as certain or proven facts, even if we think they are so. This applies to much interpretation of iconographic symbolism. All scholars can agree that a certain image had a certain meaning for people of a certain time, place, and creed. They will disagree if that meaning is stated as something divinely established, true on a higher plane of reality, or attached to the image by the very nature of things.

To be sure, no idea can be detached from its cultural context without changing it somehow. It may take on a very different meaning, as does the concept of "nature" in various philosophic systems. But some persistent nuclei of meaning can usually be preserved. The whole history of European philosophy is a never-ending process of detaching particular concepts from their original settings, as in Greek philosophy, and then recombining them with new ideas as parts of a new system. Thus the concepts of beauty and goodness, defined in many ways, reappear in the most divergent systems. The result of recombination may be an eclectic patchwork or a genuine synthesis.[147]

[147] On the requirements for a philosophic and cultural synthesis between East and West, see F. S. C. Northrop, *The Meeting of East and West* (New York, Macmillan, 1946), esp. Ch. XII. Professor Northrop's analysis of both civilizations is oversimplified as to the "aesthetic" aspects of Oriental culture and the "theoretic" aspects of Occidental. He uses the term "aesthetic" too broadly to cover almost all

My own attempts at systematic study of Indian aesthetics began in the nineteen-thirties, and the essays of Ananda Coomaraswamy were my principal guide. We met and tried to discuss aesthetics, but could not establish much communication because each of us used certain basic terms with different meanings, and there was not enough time to find a common vocabulary. In reading his more philosophical essays on art, I was often repelled by his calm assurance that his own Asiatic philosophy, the "perennial philosophy," was also "the true philosophy." I was surprised and repelled by his failure to understand or appreciate Western art and aesthetics since the Renaissance. Though often on the point of throwing his books aside, I fortunately disobeyed that impulse. Whenever he wrote of Indian art and of the ideas behind it, I felt the authority of a deeply learned connoisseur and scholar. His knowledge of Indian art was based on long, direct experience and keen observation. Some of his earlier writings are much less mystical than his later ones. There was a broad level of empirical knowledge on which I could follow him without falling into metaphysical disputes. From him I learned some of the fascinating symbolism of Indian art, as in his classic interpretation of *The Dance of Siva*. The fact that he believed some ideas to be literally or symbolically true which, for me, had no factual truth whatever, no longer troubled me. Our standards of value in art were different, but there was a common ground. At least, we could agree in respecting the wisdom of the East and its artistic expressions, as great achievements of the human hand and mind.

I think it is mere self-delusion to suppose that the Orien-

---

the immediate, directly intuited sensory components of experience. Also, he makes a questionable identification of "aesthetic" with "spiritual," as in saying "it is precisely this ineffable, emotional, moving [aesthetic] quale that constitutes what is meant by spirit and the spiritual."

tal and Occidental world-views, including their conceptions of art, can be easily reconciled. This is a delusion to which many scholars on both sides have succumbed in the warm glow of cordial East-West conferences. It is easy to say that World Unity can be achieved if the other side will accept the profound, spiritual truth *of my beliefs*. It is easy to say that Western naturalism can be reconciled with Eastern spiritualism, simply by saying that one is true on the low, empirical level and the other on the high, spiritual level. This ignores the naturalistic insistence that there is no separate, independent, spiritual realm. These are issues on which the two world-views, if clearly and frankly stated, are radically contradictory. Both cannot be true at once, and I think more is lost than gained by trying to gloss the difference over.

Such areas of radical disagreement exist in aesthetics also. The first step needed is a clearer demarcation of the areas of comparative agreement and disagreement, as well as of outlying fields where both sides can join in fruitful research and experiment. When all competing theories are placed in the arena of world opinion, we can then see which best survive the test of time. That test must include, not only intellectual argument, but practical application in art and other areas of life.

Index